M THE LIGH... ...E WOR...

SHEPHERD ...S

Y, THE TRUTH, AND THE LIF...

READ OF LIFE ✝ I AM THE L...

R ✝ I AM THE GOOD SHEPHE...

LIFE ✝ I AM THE WAY, THE...

UE VINE ✝ I AM THE BREAD...

RLD ✝ I AM THE DOOR ✝ I A...

RESURRECTION AND THE L...

HE LIFE ✝ I AM THE TRUE V...

IE LIGHT OF THE WORLD ✝...

HERD ✝ I AM THE RESURRE...

E TRUTH, AND THE LIFE ✝...

OF LIFE ✝ I AM THE LIGHT...

AM THE BREAD OF LIFE + I

HE DOOR + I AM THE GOOD

ND THE LIFE + I AM THE W

HE TRUE VINE + I AM THE

HE WORLD + I AM THE DOO

HE RESURRECTION AND TH

ND THE LIFE + I AM THE T

I AM THE LIGHT OF THE W

OOD SHEPHERD + I AM THE

HE WAY, THE TRUTH, AND

HE BREAD OF LIFE + I AM

OOR + I AM THE GOOD SHE

HE LIFE + I AM THE WAY, T

RUE VINE + I AM THE BREA

LOVED TO LIFE

ANN VOSKAMP

Illustrated by Stephen Crotts

LOVED
TO
LIFE

A 40-Day Pilgrimage with Love Himself
That Will Change Your Life

TYNDALE
MOMENTUM®

A Tyndale nonfiction imprint

Visit Tyndale online at tyndale.com.

Visit Tyndale Momentum online at tyndalemomentum.com.

Visit the author at annvoskamp.com.

Tyndale, Tyndale's quill logo, *Tyndale Momentum*, and the Tyndale Momentum logo are registered trademarks of Tyndale House Ministries. Tyndale Momentum is a nonfiction imprint of Tyndale House Publishers, Carol Stream, Illinois.

Loved to Life: A 40-Day Pilgrimage with Love Himself That Will Change Your Life

Designed by Julie Chen

Edited by Stephanie Rische

Published in association with William K. Jensen Literary Agency, 119 Bampton Court, Eugene, Oregon 97404.

All Scripture quotations, unless otherwise indicated, are taken from the Holy Bible, *New International Version,*® *NIV.*® Copyright © 1973, 1978, 1984, 2011 by Biblica, Inc.® Used by permission. All rights reserved worldwide.

Scripture quotations marked ESV are from The ESV® Bible (The Holy Bible, English Standard Version®), copyright © 2001 by Crossway, a publishing ministry of Good News Publishers. Used by permission. All rights reserved.

Scripture quotations marked MSG are taken from *The Message*, copyright © 1993, 2002, 2018 by Eugene H. Peterson. Used by permission of NavPress. All rights reserved. Represented by Tyndale House Publishers.

Scripture quotations marked NLT are taken from the *Holy Bible*, New Living Translation, copyright © 1996, 2004, 2015 by Tyndale House Foundation. Used by permission of Tyndale House Publishers, Carol Stream, Illinois 60188. All rights reserved.

Scripture quotations marked NRSV are taken from the New Revised Standard Version Bible, copyright © 1989 National Council of the Churches of Christ in the United States of America. Used by permission. All rights reserved worldwide.

Scripture quotations marked RSV are taken from the Revised Standard Version of the Bible, copyright © 1946, 1952, and 1971 National Council of the Churches of Christ in the United States of America. Used by permission. All rights reserved worldwide.

Scripture quotations marked KJV are taken from the *Holy Bible*, King James Version.

Scripture quotations marked NKJV are taken from the New King James Version,® copyright © 1982 by Thomas Nelson, Inc. Used by permission. All rights reserved.

Scripture quotations marked AMP are taken from the Amplified® Bible, copyright © 2015 by The Lockman Foundation. Used by permission. www.Lockman.org.

The URLs in this book were verified prior to publication. The publisher is not responsible for content in the links, links that have expired, or websites that have changed ownership after that time.

For information about special discounts for bulk purchases, please contact Tyndale House Publishers at csresponse@tyndale.com, or call 1-855-277-9400.

Printed in China

31	30	29	28	27	26	25
7	6	5	4	3	2	1

To one of those in the generation who came before:
Bill Jensen, whose steadying, cruciform love has deeply impacted my life
and countless lives, because his life has pointed to Life Himself.

And to all our beloveds of the generation who come behind,
to each of our grandchildren:

Only one life, 'twill soon be past,
Only what's done for Christ will last.

Live for Jesus, live for Jesus. He came to give us life,
the realest Life to the full.

CONTENTS

INTRODUCTION

THE DIVINE STEPPED into time—God knows what it feels like to be where you are, where you have been.

God Himself has been bruised and beaten up by this busted-up old world.

God has tasted the bitterness of disappointment.

He has looked into the abyss of abandonment.

God groans.

God sickens in the face of sickness and death.

Is there any way out of all this, to really live the fullest life?

God knows how hard this broken planet is, and God knows you are but dust.

But it was dust He caressed into the shape of a soul; it was dust He leaned low over and kissed to life with the warmth of one divine, holy kiss. And out of the grime of the dust, began the only love story that can break through time and go on forever.

You—*you*—are loved to death and back to the realest, most fulfilling life. This is the truest story in the whole universe. He is the only One who has ever loved you to death and came to resurrect you into the life you always hoped for. Only the passion of God has ever loved you like this, and He means for nothing less than for you to wholly experience being loved to life in all its fullness! (John 10:10, GNT).

In the Garden of Gethsemane, before Jesus went to the Passion Tree at Calvary, He rent open His heart, and this King of the universe literally sweat drops of blood over the agony of dying like this. But why would He face death like this?

Socrates faced his own death without flinching, valiantly swigging his cup of poisonous hemlock. The ancient Israelite King Saul demanded to be run through with a sword, and when his subject refused, he thrust his own soft abdomen onto the glinting sharp point himself.

Perpetua of Carthage, a new convert who was thrown into the amphitheater because of her faith, faced a wild beast with these final words: "Stand fast in the faith, and love one another, all of you, and be not offended at my sufferings."[1] Then she died on the edge of the gladiator's sword.

But God—who breathed and birthed stars in the deepest, darkest recesses of the universe—"began to be deeply distressed" in the Garden of Gethsemane before the cross: "My soul is overwhelmed with sorrow to the point of death" (Mark 14:33-34).

Why would God, the source of all life, writhe away, reeling at the jarring precipice of death?

Because what the triune God, in the person of Jesus, faced wasn't only death, like Perpetua or Saul or Socrates faced. What the triune God, in the person of Jesus, tasted in the murky shadows of the Garden of Gethsemane, what He absorbed and swallowed right down and metabolized, was all the brokenness, all the darkness, all the sadness that has ever existed in every atom, every second, every iota of the whole of the universe—and in your own heart.

In the face of pain and betrayal, God agonized. Never doubt: God understands where you are, and God knows what it's like to be you. The *vulnerability* of this kind of God proves the *reliability* of this kind of story.

Jesus held the cup that holds the story you never wanted; Jesus held the cup that holds the darkness you never wanted to know, the pain you wish you and your people had escaped, the scars that have forever marred your only heart.

And He vulnerably whisper-aches, "Take this cup of suffering away from me" (Luke 22:42, NLT), because Jesus knows the cup of suffering you've had to drink, and He knows exactly how you've felt.

Before Jesus ever suckled milk as a babe, He knew He finally would drink the bitterest cup as a love sacrifice for you (Matthew 17:22-23; Luke 9:22; Matthew 20:22-23). Before Jesus ever breathed life on this planet, He knew the sacrificial plan of how He would die for you (Ephesians 1:4; Revelation 13:8). And yet Jesus held the singular cup of suffering that contained more ache than anyone has ever known, a cup that no one else has ever had to hold, because He has to hold you and carry all you've ever had to hold.

And even more than that, the cup in Jesus' hand is the cup that holds all the holy heartbreak of God against all the hellish wrong in the world—all the righting, divine justice of God against all the unfair darkness of the world and all you've ever had to swallow.

With the mouth of the cup to His lips, God peered into the mouth of hell and into everything you've ever been ashamed of or desperately wished you'd done differently. And standing at the rim of the raging inferno, the triune God tilted back the rim of that scorching cup, because His passion for you burned greater.

If the sight of this cup of suffering distressed even this supernatural God-Man, what would have made Him drink such a great agony except His deeper and even greater supernatural love for you?

For the love of you . . . Jesus was willing to drink "to the dregs the bowl of staggering" (Isaiah 51:17, RSV).

For the love of you . . . Jesus voluntarily drank this cup down. Jesus didn't do so ignorantly, accidentally, or obliviously, stumbling into drinking it—though He staggered when He tasted the agony of it. He drank it down *because He wanted to love you back to life.*

Jesus wasn't cornered into taking the cup; He voluntarily poured out all of Himself because He wanted nothing more than to breathe life into your eternal lungs, to revive your heart with exuberant hope. The horror He foretasted in the Garden, He drank to the dregs on the Cross, knowing fully what it was, because of His uncompromising, unparalleled, life-to-the-full kind of love for you.

For the love of you and for all who came before you and for all who will come after you and for all of humanity that ever was and ever will be, His heart is rent wide open—and before Him all of hell has opened right up. And there in His hand is the pit, the abyss, the flaming precipice of the cup. And God chose to swallow it all because He chose you, kissing all your wounds until they are healed with unfathomable, perfect wholeness.

He did for you what you could never do for yourself—He laid down Himself in the impossible gap between where you are and where perfection is. And the distance you could never cover, He covers with Himself.

Loving you to death and back to life again would cost God all of God.

But Jesus made Himself your substitute, because in His eyes, nothing in all the universe could be a substitute for you. You'll find the love you've been looking for your whole life when you turn and gaze on the One who gave you His whole life.

In the midst of a world of crisis after crisis, the ultimate crisis facing your soul is now over—because the perfection of Jesus is now over you. The perfect arms of Jesus are under you, carrying you over the entire distance, so you can rest in very perfection Himself. You don't have to wait for a perfect life to have a happy life, because Jesus already gave you His perfect life—and He is all the perfection you'll ever need.

Done.

Finished.

Complete.

Arrived.

You have truly arrived when your whole life is a pilgrimage with God.

Embark on this pilgrimage over the next forty days, a pilgrimage with Jesus through the expanse of the book of John, and see His expansive, bare heart of love for you—a love that will move you from barely getting through to passionately living the fullest life.

YOU DON'T HAVE
TO WAIT FOR
A PERFECT LIFE TO
HAVE A HAPPY LIFE,
BECAUSE JESUS
ALREADY
GAVE YOU HIS
PERFECT LIFE—
AND HE IS ALL
THE PERFECTION
YOU'LL EVER NEED.

DAY
1

THE LONG ARM OF LOVE

In the beginning was the Word, and the Word was with God, and the Word was God. He was with God in the beginning. Through him all things were made; without him nothing was made that has been made. In him was life, and that life was the light of all mankind. The light shines in the darkness, and the darkness has not overcome it. . . .

The Word became flesh and made his dwelling among us. We have seen his glory . . .

JOHN 1:1-5, 14

Day *1: In the beginning was the Word. John 1:1*

IN THE BEGINNING was the glory of the Word, which literally means the *logos* of God, the logic of God that breathed life into the likes of dust like us.

The logic of God took on skin and moved, not into ivory towers, nor into social systems, nor into the upper echelons of power, but into *us*, who are but dust. Because comfort is never found in answers. Comfort is found in arms.

The logic of God became flesh, and Jesus entered into time as a baby, born with arms reaching up from a manger. And even now, He holds the whole world in His hands, dying with arms wholly extended.

The logic of God—the Word, Jesus—doesn't offer cold answers. He offers us who are but dust His warm arms, right next to His heart, to revive our hearts.

Answers are rigid, unmovable things. But arms? Arms can reach out to defend you. Arms are weapons against adversity. Arms can move around you and hold you. Arms will give you *with*ness, which is what you ache for most.

For us who are but vulnerable dust, for us who live in a wildly hard world, facing all kinds of wildly hard situations, what gives life is this relief: You don't have to take up arms to defend yourself, because Jesus takes you in His arms. Jesus is how you bear arms against the dark, against discouragement, against despair, and against the devil. Jesus' arms can genuinely move you . . . and they can genuinely carry you. Every warrior knows it: It's arms that can carry you through to victory.

And though you are but dust, you can feel it now: Underneath you are not lonely stretches of wilderness, nor abysses of despair, nor the rubble of ruined dreams—underneath you "are the everlasting arms" of Love Himself (Deuteronomy 33:27).

When you tear back every doubt, strip back every haunting question, and get to the foundation under everything, that's what is underneath everything: God's everlasting arms.

Everything else can cut you loose; everything else can cut you deep, can be cut away. But underneath you still are God's everlasting arms. And when you are at your lowest, still underneath you are His arms, which will go to any length to hold you.

When you fall, you fall into His everlasting arms—and you can never fall through them.

The long arm of Love will always catch you, always find you and truly free you. No suffering, no ache, no pain, no loss can outlast His everlasting arms. Whatever your depths, the depths of His divine love for you are deeper yet.

Make no mistake: Evil is a snake that writhes through the dust with no arms, and with no arms, evil can win no battles. Jesus has crushed the snake's head and disarmed evil forever, and because evil has no arms, there is nothing in all this dark universe that can ever snatch you away from the safe arms of Jesus.

The Word became flesh, and Jesus has arms—arms He stretched out on a Cross to find you, to reach you, to embrace you, to slay the dark so He could win and save you. His love for you is forever nailed down and going nowhere.

Sharp doubts and disappointments may grab and pull at you, but they have no arms to grab hold of you. Grief may stalk close, but it has no arms to keep you in its grip. The only thing that holds in all this world is God, who came with arms, the curves of your name cut right into His hands (Isaiah 49:16).

It's only Christ's arms that can arm you for life's battle. Whatever very real battle you're in, you're in the very arms of Christ. Christ's arms are the only place you win peace.

Feel how His affection for you is disproportionate to the afflictions facing you. Whatever the depths of your affliction, greater are the depths of His affection. Be still in His arms, settled and safe and steadied and soothed.

What your soul has sought the most is to be sought out. And when you lay back and rest in His arms, you can look into His eyes and see that everything you've been looking for has always been looking deeply into you.

You are but dust, and you are small and finite, and to dust you will return. But it's true: When you rest in His arms and look up, you see that you are seen. Love Himself would have to cease to be if He ever ceased loving you.

In the beginning, you began as dust, and in the beginning was the

Word, and the Word was with God, and the Word Himself is with you now. And through Him all things are made, and you were made, and you are being remade right now—by Love, for love.

Though you are but dust, *in Him is life*. Though you are dying to self, His life and His love come to dwell *right within you*. And though you will know wildernesses, you will be held with love, *by Love Himself*.

Though you are but dust, you will see His glory. Only Christ's love can disarm everything coming against you.

This is the first step of your pilgrimage into being loved to life: Rest in His arms, gaze into His face, and feel the beat of His heart for you.

PERSONAL NOTES TO SOUL FROM TODAY'S PILGRIMAGE INTO THE HEART OF JESUS:

REST IN

HIS ARMS

BECAUSE ONLY

CHRIST'S LOVE

CAN DISARM

EVERYTHING

COMING

AGAINST YOU.

DAY
2

BEHOLD

The next day John saw Jesus coming toward him and said, "Look! The Lamb of God who takes away the sin of the world! He is the one I was talking about when I said, 'A man is coming after me who is far greater than I am, for he existed long before me.' I did not recognize him as the Messiah, but I have been baptizing with water so that he might be revealed to Israel."

JOHN 1:29-31, NLT

Day 2: "Look! The Lamb of God who takes away the sin of the world!" John 1:29

WHEN WE CAN'T LIFT the weight of our broken hearts, the weight of our burdens, the weight of being us, all there is to do is lift our eyes—only our eyes—to the Lamb of God.

He offers His own back to lift and shoulder it all. Only the Lamb of God has a back equal to whatever burden we bear. He is the Brokenhearted Bearer of the World.

The lifting of eyes to look to the Lamb of God—this is lifting that even the weariest among us can do. And yet, in the paradox of all things true, the way we turn our eyes may actually be the hardest of all.

Because focusing the eyes is always a matter of how we focus the heart.

Where the eyes are fixed, so the heart is. Where the looking goes, so the heart goes. *Where you look is where you love.*

Looking to what your hands can do, looking to what your work is working on, looking to what all your striving is reaching for does little to no good at all. You don't have to know what to do, but just decide: Lord, Lamb of God, "our eyes are on you" (2 Chronicles 20:12).

Where you look will save—or smother—your life.

Behold your Lamb, who holds nothing against you but only holds you against His heart, so you can let go and hold nothing back from Him. Lucky in love are all of us whose unspoken broken is forgiven, whose failures are taken away by the One who takes away all the sins of the world, because He is so taken with you, His beloved (Psalm 32:1; Hebrews 10:4).

Before the foundation of the world was ever laid, here is your Lamb, who laid down His life because of His everlasting love for you. Before one step was ever taken out of the Garden of Eden, here is your Lamb, who, there in the Garden, stepped forward to give Himself to cover all your nakedness and brokenness. Before our father Abraham sacrificed his only son, here is your Lamb, who offered Himself as the only begotten One to be our substitution, our provision, our restitution, our soul revolution, our absolution, and our ultimate solution. Before any wails passed the lips of Egypt over the death of its firstborns, here is your Lamb, who sacrificed Himself for every doorframe so the angel of death might pass over all God's children with a kiss of undying grace. Before every Levitical priest with cleansing on his mind, here is your Lamb, who laid bare His vulnerable heart, slain with love for you. Before the shearers, here is your Lamb, who was silent because His love was speaking the loudest of all, silencing every lie that you aren't worth being loved back to the fullest life.

Here is your Lamb, Love laid down, right before you. He is looking into your eyes to see if you are looking for Him.

What should have more preeminence than looking toward our Lamb, who slays our every lion?

But the human eye tends to be drawn toward wherever a hole has been drawn.

It's the way the human eye turns—we look toward loss, fixated on what we can't fix. The eyes of the heart are drawn to absences. We look toward loss because our interior health is ultimately a function of how we see loss, process loss, live in spite of loss, live through endless loss. How we view our losses determines how we brave our life.

How do we look at our losses and keep on fully living? Look, behold— the Lamb of God who takes away all the wrongness and darkness and sinfulness, who takes it all so we can actually know the loss of all we've desperately wanted to shake off. Behold the Lamb, who takes away all we've wanted gone, so none of our burdens or losses can ever outweigh our great gain *in Him*.

The Lamb who takes away everything wrong for us—He is worthy to take everything in our hands as our offering of thanks:

> *The slain Lamb is worthy!*
> *Take the power, the wealth, the wisdom, the strength!*
> *Take the honor, the glory, the blessing!*

REVELATION 5:12, MSG

Behold, the Lamb of God, who takes away all the darkness to take us to Himself, to see us, to know us, to hold us.

When you keep beholding the Lamb of God, who takes away the sins of the world, you have what it takes to keep going—because He takes you. One holy step after the other, on a pilgrimage into the only Love that wholly revives.

PERSONAL NOTES TO SOUL FROM TODAY'S PILGRIMAGE INTO THE HEART OF JESUS:

WHERE THE

EYES ARE FIXED,

SO THE HEART

IS. WHERE YOU

LOOK IS WHERE

YOU LOVE.

IN HIS EYES

The next day John was there again with two of his disciples. When he saw Jesus passing by, he said, "Look, the Lamb of God!" When the two disciples heard him say this, they followed Jesus. Turning around, Jesus saw them following and asked, "What do you want?"

JOHN 1:35-38

Day 3: *"What do you want?" John 1:38*

And this kind of detail, which carefully notes that it was just the next day that John saw Jesus passing by, means that this is nothing less than a detailed eyewitness account of the God who is Love coming down to us. It's only an actual eyewitness account of seeing the Divine Himself that could bear witness to these time-of-day details.

This story is not the stuff of legend, this is the stuff of literality, the stuff of life and love—the stuff that can be told only if looked on with one's very own eyes. Why would writers of Jewish descent, who categorically believed that the name of God, YHWH, was too holy to be spoken aloud, whip around to make up any deliberate lie that their hallowed God took on marrow, pulled on skin, and moved in next door and into the chambers of our hearts? Why would they willingly be martyred and die for such a wild lie? Either this is all an elaborate ruse or this is all the passion of God, the Divine who stepped into time to defy logic and love us beyond time.

Either countless people chose to die for a lie they said they saw with their own two eyes or the God of the cosmos slipped on humanity and into history and loved us to death and then right back to fullest life.

John says in his account of Jesus, "Behold!" Behold the Word! Behold the Lamb! To which Jesus responded with His very first recorded statement in the Gospel of John: "Come!"

In John's honest-to-God account, the very first words out of the mouth of God on this sod was the question, "What do you want?" And the invitation, "Come and you will see."

Jesus wants to know what you want—and He wants you to come and see that everything He is, is everything you really want.

What do you really want?

Do you dare to come and see Him and believe that once you behold Him, you will come to Him, because He is really what you want most?

When you want Him most, when you come to see Him, you will leave things behind to be with Him. It may be possible to behold the Lamb anywhere, but you can't be a disciple of the Lord until you leave things behind and come to be with Him. Thirty times throughout his sacred writings, including the book of Revelation, John points to the Lord of all as the

Lamb of God, because it's beholding the Lamb in our hardest times that can hold our lives together all the time. But the pilgrimage into the fullest life is more than only beholding the Lamb of God, who takes away all the sin of your world, and taking Him merely as an all-access pass to heaven instead of as Lord over all your passions, who is your greatest passion. It's one thing to follow someone's thoughts and ideas tracked across a stage or social media, and you may applaud their insights that have focused your sights on better horizons, and their way of thinking may have changed the way you live. But following someone's platform isn't the same as what it's like to follow someone to the matrimonial altar and give them your life, which changes everything about your life. (Of all the images painted for us in the Word to capture Jesus' relationship with us, one of the most tender of all is the image of Jesus as our Bridegroom, and us as His beloved, His bride [Luke 5:33-35; Revelation 21:2].)

And ascribing to someone's beliefs isn't the same as scribing their name on your ring finger and giving them your life. You can *believe* in someone but not be committed to them as your *beloved*. When you're committed to someone, when you become one with someone, you don't just applaud them and tell them that they're great, like some social media follow. You tell them *everything*—you tell them the gritty and intimate and everyday details of your life, and everyone can tell you're together. There's actually a world of difference between ascribing to someone's belief and pledging allegiance to someone's life. Pledging allegiance to someone is going to cost you something—*maybe everything.*

When you behold the Lamb of God, who takes away the sins of the world, He will take you and challenge you to not only watch Him but *walk with Him.* Those who truly behold Him will be held to nothing less than *discipleship.*

A true disciple's life testifies that all other loves are secondary to love for Christ, because of His all-encompassing passion for His beloved.

You only know what it means to live as a disciple when you live into the art of discipline, the art of surrendering your present desires so you can receive the gift of an even greater passion. Because the truth is, if you are driven by your passions, you will lose your life. But if you lose your passions in a greater passion for Jesus, you will find the greatest love . . . and your greatest life.

There has to be more than just believing, because even the demons believe. This is the only way to be a real believer: Believers behold Him and then become disciples. Jesus isn't looking for believers who merely believe in Him; He's looking for disciples who are in love with Him, who stand with Him, who live with Him.

Discipleship is a function of relationship; the more robust our *relationship* with Christ, the more robust our *discipleship* in Christ. The *intimacy* of our relationship determines the *efficacy* of our discipleship.

After we behold our Lamb, whose eyes are gentle, tender, full of consolation and compassion, we want to come and see, and keep seeing—but the temptation can be to divert, to distract, to turn our eyes toward what we think will be easy on our eyes, what will be easier on us, what will let our souls rest easier.

Too often it's true: The temptation can be to look away from Him, in other directions, because we feel little to no attraction. That we could feel little—or even worse, that we could feel avoidance in the presence of His infinite, incomparable glory—this is a confession of great grief. And there are other times when the gaze of God can ignite a guilt that scorches the soul, a fire of failure. But it's even truer: If there's even the merest cry for help in our eyes, there is a rescuing, glorious *yes* in His eyes that extinguishes all fear.

Nowhere is easier to look in all the universe than into the eyes of the Lamb.

In His eyes, you won't find one who disowns you, only One who delights in you. In His eyes, you won't find any rejection, only unending passion, to love you into the realest life. He is holy, and He is wholly Love. Do not fear His gaze, but hold His gaze and feel His pure love burn away all the dross, purifying and holding you. Opening your eyes to Him is opening your deepest self to Him—and being open to receive the acceptance that your whole life has been looking for and the transformation you have always hoped for. No one looks into the eyes of Love and stays the same. Look into the eyes of a love that sacrifices for you, that lives to give to you, that surrenders for you, that covers you, that sustains you, that always and unconditionally carries you—and you will commit your life and death to love the same.

Here is a place to linger: Jesus Christ's love to see you exceeds even your own ache to be seen. His eyes are full of compassion for you—and that compassion is the very passage to complete change within you. Being united with Him is being whole.

And that question of what it means to be a disciple of Jesus, to be a pilgrim on this pilgrim's road, can be answered only with every moment of your life.

Grace is free, but discipleship will cost—and God is infinitely worthy.

PERSONAL NOTES TO SOUL FROM TODAY'S PILGRIMAGE INTO THE HEART OF JESUS:

COME AND SEE

When he saw Jesus passing by, he said, "Look, the Lamb of God!" When the two disciples heard him say this, they followed Jesus. Turning around, Jesus saw them following and asked, "What do you want?" They said, "Rabbi" (which means Teacher), "where are you staying?" "Come," he replied, "and you will see."

JOHN 1:35-39

Day 4: *"Come . . . and you will see."* John 1:39

Jesus says to you in this moment, "Come and see," because Jesus knows that whatever you see, *you can't unsee.*

Once you've witnessed, traced, touched, grazed a bit of His glory, once you've intimately known someone, you can't ultimately *unknow* them.

Critics may lob all kinds of arguments to discredit God, and skeptics may bandy around a whole bunch of doubts about God, and experts may expect all their lofty suppositions to move you to some other perspective, but the undeniable truth is, once you've experienced God, you can't unexperience Him.

No argument about God can argue with an experience of God.

"What do you want? . . . Come and see," Jesus says, because Jesus wants your eyes.

Because: What you gaze on is what you fall in love with.

Stare at screens and streams long enough and all you can fall in love with is an image of self or stuff. But genuinely beholding Him always leads to following Him.

The passion of the Lamb ultimately asks, *What do you really want most?*

Do you want the things that will fade or the things that are forever? Do you want the expendable things or the eternal things? Do you want the things that will fill the hollows in you with stress or serenity? The second hand of every clock claps, claps, claps it: *What do you want? What do you want? What do you want?*

Isn't our deepest wanting always for things otherworldly?

Who merely wants what glitters and shimmers and blows away, sparkling flecks in the wind? The heart longs for the things of solidity for all eternity, the rock-steady things that will anchor you in any headwind and will survive fire, flame, and all evil's ferocity.

This is a world of loves, but there is only one love that can be soul-sustenance, only one love story that can sustain your soul—solely the passion for Love Himself.

Who but Jesus is really dying to know you? Who but Jesus has ever wanted to know you at the expense of His very life? Who but Jesus would pay such a high price to love you to death and back to fullest life? It's true:

You love as well as you are willing to be inconvenienced—and who has been more inconvenienced in their love for you than the one who laid down His life for you?

When someone desperately wants to know all of you, you desperately want more of that—and Jesus wants to know you, every iota of you, all of you, and His love for you is limitless, boundless, bottomless, all the way up to the very heights of heaven.

The One whose mind knows how to choreograph all the stars and planets across the swirling stage of the sky—He gave His very lifeblood to know all of your life, to be the center that holds all of your life.

All the millions of sacrificial lambs in the Old Testament that were the safe covering for tattered, tarnished lives over millennia—they were all pointing to this Lamb. All the stories of the Old Testament were pointing to this love story. All the stories in this world are ultimately giving their commentary on the story of the Word, and all the words in the world are ultimately wrestling with this Word. Every one of the world's stories is either trashing or treasuring this Word and His story.

And the Word Himself lives the story you should have lived, and dies the death your story should have had, all to write you into the cosmic love story you were made for—the story of His passion, the story of His love sacrificing for you.

There's a way into this story that is better than all the legends, because this is literal reality.

There's a way into this story that is better than any story on a larger-than-life or handheld screen, because this is the story that comes and saves you.

And the way into this story isn't dependent on anything you have to do or perform for or strive for—the way into the story is gazing into the infinite love of God.

The way into this story is looking into the tender face of the One who offers you His hand and says, "I am the door" and then opens wide His life to give you His heart and be the way into the Kingdom of God and living fully alive.

This is the pilgrimage into everything you've ever wanted to come and see and experience in your life.

PERSONAL NOTES TO SOUL FROM TODAY'S PILGRIMAGE INTO THE HEART OF JESUS:

WHO

BUT JESUS

WOULD PAY

SUCH A HIGH

PRICE TO LOVE

YOU TO DEATH

AND BACK TO

FULLEST LIFE?

THIRSTY FOR GOD

Jesus also was invited to the wedding with his disciples. When the wine ran out, the mother of Jesus said to him, "They have no wine." And Jesus said to her, "Woman, what does this have to do with me? My hour has not yet come." His mother said to the servants, "Do whatever he tells you."

Now there were six stone water jars there for the Jewish rites of purification, each holding twenty or thirty gallons. Jesus said to the servants, "Fill the jars with water." And they filled them up to the brim. And he said to them, "Now draw some out and take it to the master of the feast." So they took it. When the master of the feast tasted the water now become wine, and did not know where it came from (though the servants who had drawn the water knew), the master of the feast called the bridegroom and said to him, "Everyone serves the good wine first, and when people have drunk freely, then the poor wine. But you have kept the good wine until now."

JOHN 2:2-10, ESV

Day 5: *"Do whatever he tells you." John 2:5*

THIS WAS THE BEGINNING of the revolution that changed the way this whole old world revolves.

This was the first literal miracle of God-with-skin-on.

This was the moment that God-with-skin-on began the revolution with a cup to swallow down all the tears and aches that leave us all downtrodden.

This taking of the stone jugs full of 150 gallons of clear water at a wedding feast and making every last drop into velvet-lush cups of the sweetest spirits—this was the first strange stirring that something otherworldly had invaded this world.

This first miracle actually fulfilled prophecy. Hadn't the prophets of old prophesied that the running of wine would be the beginning of the revolution to wipe away every tear running down cheeks? "On this mountain the LORD of hosts will make for all peoples a feast of rich food, a feast of well-aged wines, of rich food filled with marrow, of well-aged wines strained clear. And he will destroy on this mountain the shroud that is cast over all peoples, . . . he will swallow up death forever. Then the LORD God will wipe away the tears from all faces, and the disgrace of his people he will take away from all the earth, for the LORD has spoken" (Isaiah 25:6-8, NRSV).

Though our tears may run, the wine of the new age has already begun to run.

This first miracle was nothing less than a formational parable.

While Jesus was a guest at this wedding, the wedding He was seeing was His own, with us who are His church, the bride. This wasn't just about a wedding in Cana and the marriage supper of two young Jews; this was really about the wedding of Jesus Christ Himself and the marriage supper of the Lamb. This wedding at Cana was actually a parable for *the wedding of Christ* with His own bride, the church.

The awe begins at the wedding.

In the whole of the Gospel of John, Jesus' mother enters the story only twice: first here, at the first miracle of turning water into wine at the wedding, and then at the Cross, the miracle of turning sinners into saints. And Mary didn't tell Jesus what to do; she only came to tell Him what had already happened. Mary entrusted the need to Jesus and trusted that Jesus would work out whatever miracle was needed.

When we are running out of hope, we don't tell Jesus how to run the world—we simply run to Jesus.

Leave the matter to Jesus, because He has proven He can change the matter of water, making a miracle out of any debacle.

And when Mary told Him that the wine had run out, Jesus told her that the hour for His dying hadn't yet come, because what He knew was this: The price He would pay for the wine served at His own wedding to His bride, to us, the church, was His own life.

The jugs that held the water He would make into wine weren't commonplace jugs. They were the stone jugs of ceremonial cleansing that held the water every Jew washed themselves with before entering the Temple and the presence of God.[1] Jesus made the cleansing water into wine, the way only His blood can cleanse our souls.

The only way to clasp us, His bride, close is for His very lifeblood to fill the Communion cup. The only way to unite with His bride is to give His own life. The Lamb slain before the foundation of the world gave Himself for complete union with you, His bride. Since the very beginning, the passion of God never intended to be only tolerant of us, or even simply befriend us; He always meant to be *betrothed to us.*

The atonement was always about "at-one-ment." God has always wanted more than to forgive us of our sins—He has always wanted to *give us Himself.* The passion of God has always wanted more than only to be with us—He has always intended to be wed to us.

This is why, at the wedding of Cana the passion of God worked Jesus' first miracle, turning water into wine, and the real miracle began to unfold—His turning to face the cross of Calvary and loving us to death and back to the realest life, which is union with Him.

As Jesus put the cup of celebrating wine to His lips, what He tasted was more than the juice of the vine. As the wine slid down, Jesus tasted the cup of His own suffering. In the Garden of Gethsemane, Jesus would beg, "Let the cup pass from me," but there was no way He would let you pass from Him. The only way He can wed us is to go through hell for us. Who has ever loved you like this? Jesus took that cup of suffering because He was committed to go to hell and back to take you as His own.

We only ever taste true joy because Jesus tasted the worst sorrow.

Swallow the sweet relief of that and taste and see how very good the Lord is, because He tasted all the very worst to be with us (Psalm 34:8).

You can sit ramrod straight and nod that you believe in the goodness of God, but that isn't in any way the same as having tasted and savored the miraculous grace of a God who drank down the dregs of your worst nightmare so you can wake to fully living fully loved.

"There is a difference between believing that God is holy and gracious, and having a new sense on the heart of the loveliness and beauty of that holiness and grace," writes Jonathan Edwards in *A Divine and Supernatural Light.* "The difference between believing that God is gracious and tasting that God is gracious is as different as having a rational belief that honey is sweet and having the actual sense of its sweetness."[2] There is a difference between believing chocolate tastes good by what you read in a textbook and coming to taste the creamy morsel melt on your desperate lips when it feels like you've been slowly starving for months.

Explaining God isn't the same as *experiencing* God, like believing in the realness of God isn't the same as actually tasting the relief of God. And whatever you've drunk down as relief, you'll crave more of. What you crave, there your soul is.

And if you're not thirsting for God, the question for the soul is, *What are you deathly drunk on that is deceptively destroying you?* Or how are you dangerously dehydrated in ways that are slowly but surely withering you to death? If you're not thirsting for God, when was the last time you sat still long enough to truly savor the richness of His love for you? You can't ever taste anything you aren't close enough to touch.

"For in this world God blesses us in such a way as to give us a mere foretaste of his kindness, and by that taste to entice us to desire heavenly blessings with which we may be satisfied," writes John Calvin.[3]

Jesus is the soul's richest wine.

This knowing Jesus is more than agreeing to some logical treatise to impress God. Knowing Jesus is about coming to a love feast to *wed* God.

The awe begins at a wedding. And when the sands of time run out right into forever, the Groom will take your hand at the marriage supper of the Lamb.

You can feel it already now: Where you're running out is right where you run to Jesus with your needs.

Where you are in short supply, Jesus meets you with a longer arm, a longer love, a longer provision.

Like the servants at the wedding at Cana were participants in the miracle, pouring the cleansing water into the stone jars, so every one of us, as Jesus' servants who willingly pour out our own hearts into Jesus' cleansing heart, can be participants in the miracle of our own transformation.

As the groom left his father's house to come for his bride, so Christ left His Father's house to come for His bride: *you.*

His pilgrimage of love to you is what moves you into a pilgrimage of love to Him—and into His infinite heart of love for you, which holds the expansive life.

PERSONAL NOTES TO SOUL FROM TODAY'S PILGRIMAGE INTO THE HEART OF JESUS:

TURNING OVER TABLES

The Passover of the Jews was at hand, and Jesus went up to Jerusalem. In the temple he found those who were selling oxen and sheep and pigeons, and the money-changers sitting there. And making a whip of cords, he drove them all out of the temple, with the sheep and oxen. And he poured out the coins of the money-changers and overturned their tables. And he told those who sold the pigeons, "Take these things away; do not make my Father's house a house of trade." His disciples remembered that it was written, "Zeal for your house will consume me."

So the Jews said to him, "What sign do you show us for doing these things?" Jesus answered them, "Destroy this temple, and in three days I will raise it up." The Jews then said, "It has taken forty-six years to build this temple, and will you raise it up in three days?" But he was speaking about the temple of his body. When therefore he was raised from the dead, his disciples remembered that he had said this, and they believed the Scripture and the word that Jesus had spoken.

Now when he was in Jerusalem at the Passover Feast, many believed in his name when they saw the signs that he was doing. But Jesus on his part did not entrust himself to them, because he knew all people and needed no one to bear witness about man, for he himself knew what was in man.

JOHN 2:13-25, ESV

Day 6: *"Do not make my Father's house a house of trade." John 2:16*

JESUS ISN'T ABOUT having you keep any cheap regulations for Him but about having you keep a wholehearted devotion toward Him, because it's His love alone that keeps you through everything.

The Passover was at hand. And Jesus knows what was in the heart of man. Passover, or Pascha, as it was called by the Jewish people during Jesus' time, is the time of year when God's people remembered how, in Egypt, the doorframes were marked with the scarlet blood of lambs so the haunting specter of the angel of death might pass over each family huddled there with hope for another day.

John, the disciple whom Jesus loved, writes of three Passovers in his Gospel, this being the first. From Cana to Capernaum and on to Jerusalem at Passover, Jesus moved from His first miracle—transforming cleansing water into wine around wedding tables—to turning over tables in a purifying cleansing of the Temple.

It is still true in this very moment: Jesus brings wine and celebration to your table, and Jesus will turn tables to bring you wholeness and sanctification.

The money-changers overturned God's place of intimate communion with His people—what God wants most. So Jesus has the right to turn the tables in the Temple, cleansing and turning hearts back to the Lover of their souls. And Jesus has the right to turn whatever tables, because this whole world turns on the axis of His words.

God will use whatever He can to drive out all perversion so you can enter into life in His presence. God throws the money-changers out of His house because God desires His own house to be a place of tender interchange and exchange with His own.

At the wedding in Cana, Jesus had said, "It's not my time yet," and at the time, Mary had said four words that are timeless: "Do whatever He says." Whatever the Word says is what we're made to incarnate.

We have agency, but Jesus alone has sovereignty.

In the Temple, Jesus said, "Take these things away; do not make my Father's house a house of trade."

We have agency, but Jesus alone has *authority*.

Jesus has the authority to take His hands—the hands that bore scars, the hands that bear the curve of our very own names etched deep into the palms—and quietly pick up and wave a whip. That whip formed out of cords was literally, according to the original Greek language, made of reeds. The Word held a whip made not of stinging leather but of the same kind of reeds used to make papyrus paper.

Just as He promised that a bruised reed He would not break (Isaiah 42:3), Jesus has never held a whip that wounds. Jesus holds a whip that holds up who He, the Word, truly is. This isn't a whip that deeply pains; this is a whip that deeply purifies. This isn't a whip that drives anyone out due to an injury; this is a whip that moves people forward because of an epiphany.

Their epiphany was that the glory of the Lamb holds all authority.

It wasn't the power of Jesus' reed whip that compelled anyone to obey—it was the power of Jesus' real passion for His people. No one stands in the very real presence and passion of Jesus and demands answers, because His presence and passion demand nothing less than real obedience.

It's a gentle good to ask our soul: If you only obey God when you understand, are you really standing with God? If you only follow God when He gives you a good enough reason, is He really good enough for you?

Is it possible that we sometimes love God less for His presence, and more to leverage Him for our benefit?

And would God actually be worthy of our standing with Him if we could always fully understand Him?

Is it possible we aren't using everything in our life as a way to move closer to God, but actually using God to move us closer to all the things we want in life?

What if the only reason you need, for all that has happened, is that He happens to be God, and He happens to be turning all the impossible things into more good than you can possibly imagine?

If, at times, we secretly harbor fury at God for not moving the world the way we want, then surely He must be worthy of our awe, because He's moving in ways beyond our understanding. *And then He is infinitely worthy of our moving closer to Him.*

What if the only reason you ever needed, in the midst of everything, is knowing who He is? God didn't show Job the answers to his questions— He showed Job Himself, the only real answer to all our quests (Job 38–42). Once you truly know who God is, you know all you truly need to know.

Jesus overturns our tables, and it may upend us, but He is worthy of turning everything over to because He is making all things right in the end. The One who fills our tables with wine, to fill us with joy, can also turn all the tables with a divine turnaround, to cleanse us from all that turns us away from Him—and then fill us with more of Himself.

Wherever Jesus is turning your tables, you can trust Him enough to turn and say: *You have the authority to do this, because Your great glory and my great good are Your greatest priorities.*

And in the midst of our world turning and our tables turning and our own hearts turning, our hearts know, like every God-follower in the Old Testament knew, the only way to come close to God is to come with a sacrifice. Yet our hearts try to avoid sacrifice, and we can try to shortcut the cost and inconvenience of the sacrifice. But why bring God a cheap sacrifice that is no sacrifice at all, a fake sacrifice that costs little to noth-ing, when Jesus' love for you drove Him to everything, His whole beating heart? Jesus Himself couldn't ever turn from the Cross He came for, and the Lamb who came to lay down His life for Love turned over tables to turn hearts around so we might ask our own hearts, *How can you go through the motions of being covered by the sacrifice of the Lamb, and not be moved by a far deeper love for the Lamb?* Can the children of God taste the cost of the sacrifice of God?

This is everything. The key to living passionately for God is to keep remembering the passion of God.

When you keep holding in your mind that He loved you to death and back to the fullest life, you hold the key to knowing how to live and love till your last breath. When the passionate sacrifice of Christ is always before you, how can you not passionately love Him back with a love that's willing to sacrifice?

Now is the moment we feel everything turn, the moment we feel Jesus Himself turning over every flimsy facade, throwing out every subtle distraction, flipping over all the cheap and easy faith, casting out every wide way that leads to disappointing pits, cleansing the heart of lesser loves.

Jesus overflows your table with wine and goodness, and Jesus overturns your tables for prayer and faithfulness, and He's driven to both because of His overwhelming passion for you.

Every pilgrimage into fully living keeps turning toward Love Himself.

PERSONAL NOTES TO SOUL FROM TODAY'S PILGRIMAGE INTO THE HEART OF JESUS:

A NEWBORN SOUL

Now there was a Pharisee, a man named Nicodemus who was a member of the Jewish ruling council. He came to Jesus at night and said, "Rabbi, we know that you are a teacher who has come from God. For no one could perform the signs you are doing if God were not with him."

Jesus replied, "Very truly I tell you, no one can see the kingdom of God unless they are born again."

"How can someone be born when they are old?" Nicodemus asked. "Surely they cannot enter a second time into their mother's womb to be born!"

Jesus answered, "Very truly I tell you, no one can enter the kingdom of God unless they are born of water and the Spirit. Flesh gives birth to flesh, but the Spirit gives birth to spirit. You should not be surprised at my saying, 'You must be born again.' The wind blows wherever it pleases. You hear its sound, but you cannot tell where it comes from or where it is going. So it is with everyone born of the Spirit."

"How can this be?" Nicodemus asked.

"You are Israel's teacher," said Jesus, "and do you not understand these things? Very truly I tell you, we speak of what we know, and we testify to what we have seen, but still you people do not accept our testimony. I have spoken to you of earthly things and you do not believe;

Day 7: *"No one can see the kingdom of God unless they are born again." John 3:3*

how then will you believe if I speak of heavenly things? No one has ever gone into heaven except the one who came from heaven—the Son of Man. Just as Moses lifted up the snake in the wilderness, so the Son of Man must be lifted up, that everyone who believes may have eternal life in him."

JOHN 3:1-15

IN A HARD WORLD of detours through deserts, again and again, the only way to keep putting one step in front of the other on this pilgrimage into the fullest life is this: to be born again.

This is a cosmic mystery from the lips of Jesus Himself—the mystery that those who are born again, get to hope again, rise again, start again, and never be the same again.

When your soul trusts Jesus to be all that His love proves Him to be, that is the moment you're delivered and truly born into the realest life. When the Holy Spirit, who moves like the mystery of wind and water, moves into the sanctuary of your soul, your soul is born again—the spiritual waters breaking, your soul breathing in the holy presence of God Himself.

This is as holy as the day any newborn soul first breathes in the air of this earth.

All the born again get new hearts and new minds, new eyes and new ears, new hands and new feet, and a new way of being in a broken world, reborn as citizens of a new Kingdom. This is no small thing: The born again get to walk in newness of life till their last moment of life here!

"Now we look inside, and what we see is that anyone united with the Messiah gets a fresh start, is created new. The old life is gone; a new life emerges! Look at it!" (2 Corinthians 5:17, MSG). Come and taste and see: Jesus didn't come so we could try harder again; Jesus came for us to be *born again*.

Does the galaxy of stars that were birthed from the words of His mouth know it too? The only kind of Christian there ever has been, is now, and ever will be, is a born-again Christian. Born-again Christians aren't a particular category of Christianity, like being "completely pregnant" isn't a particular category of pregnancy. There is no other way to actually be a Christian. If you want to be a true Christian, you must truly be born again. This is what Jesus said—not once, not twice, but thrice. This way of rebirth has always been the only way to be on *the Way.*

"Then I grasped that the justice of God is that righteousness by which through grace and sheer mercy God justifies us through faith. . . . I felt myself to be reborn and to have gone through open doors into paradise" is how the preeminent theologian Martin Luther described his own profound rebirth experience.[1]

When you taste how you're a dead soul walking, you don't write off being born again as ludicrous, because being born again is your only hope. This is the mystery of rebirth—a supernatural remaking of all things interior, a hallowed and miraculous renewal within, God remaking our DNA so divine Love Himself is in our genes.

Nicodemus had only come seeking a new teacher, not a new birth. But there isn't any kind of learning that can resuscitate ashen corpses. Jesus didn't come to merely inform us; Jesus came to completely transform us. When you're dead as a doornail, you don't need more learning—what you need is new life, found in the One who came to be the door to your rebirth.

Why would we just want some self-help instructor when Jesus wants selfless intimacy? He knows our souls need more than some cheap five-point plan with a money-back guarantee if you're not completely satisfied in thirty days. Our souls need Someone guaranteed to endlessly pay attention to the aching longings of our heart, then pay the price with the only sacrifice that satisfies to birth us into a family of Love. When the cosmic amniotic fluids of the Spirit move in us and we are moved to be born again, divine Love becomes part of who we actually are. Only the mystery of being reborn into Love's family can transform our souls—and bring us to life.

Yet how does a soul know if it has been genuinely, mysteriously born again?

"Well, it is not whether or not the person has had conviction of sin or not. People can have conviction of sin and never be regenerate," wrote Jonathan Edwards. "It is not whether conversion is fast, speedy. Stony ground hearers receive the Word immediately. It is not whether when people profess to be converted they have physical phenomena, they tremble or weep. No. . . . It is none of these things. The real evidence of conversion is the presence of regeneration and regeneration is a change of nature, a new life."[2] What Jonathan Edwards ultimately offers is that a genuine Christ-follower is nothing less than "a new creature, he is just as if he were not the same, but were born again, created over a second time."[3]

Like a newborn babe keeps looking for the face looking for her, so every soul knows it has been reborn when, in a world of distractions, it keeps looking toward the Father, seeking the Father's smile, meeting the Father's smile with wild delight. Our home is in His eyes.

Like a newborn's paramount priority, moment by moment, is to attach to her caregiver, knowing she's dependent on her caregiver for everything that will keep her truly alive, you know you're reborn when your paramount priority is to keep turning toward your Abba Father, seeking from Him what will keep you alive. You know you're reborn when you keep reaching to attach to your Father, looking where He looks in the world, talking like He talks, imitating what He does.

Life in Christ isn't about moral reformation for Christ; life in Christ is about total *regeneration* through Christ.

The Spirit stirs our soul-waters with new life, and new faith isn't self-generated but first Spirit-generated. "The person without the Spirit does not accept the things that come from the Spirit of God but considers them foolishness, and cannot understand them because they are discerned only through the Spirit," the Book testifies (1 Corinthians 2:14).

Because the Christ-life simply isn't doable. It's actually impossible— unless Christ gives a dead person life, new life—*His* life.

Just as no person ever controlled how or when they were born, no person controls how they are born again; being born again is a work of God alone.

The spiritual life is a product of the Spirit, not a striving life.

Feel it happening right now, here on this sacred pilgrimage: the Spirit hovering over the surface of your soul, stirring within you—delivering you into newness of life.

PERSONAL NOTES TO SOUL FROM TODAY'S PILGRIMAGE INTO THE HEART OF JESUS:

SOUL PARCHED

When a Samaritan woman came to draw water, Jesus said to her, "Will you give me a drink?" (His disciples had gone into the town to buy food.)

The Samaritan woman said to him, "You are a Jew and I am a Samaritan woman. How can you ask me for a drink?" (For Jews do not associate with Samaritans.)

Jesus answered her, "If you knew the gift of God and who it is that asks you for a drink, you would have asked him and he would have given you living water."

"Sir," the woman said, "you have nothing to draw with and the well is deep. Where can you get this living water? Are you greater than our father Jacob, who gave us the well and drank from it himself, as did his sons and his livestock?"

Jesus answered, "Everyone who drinks this water will be thirsty again, but whoever drinks the water I give them will never thirst. Indeed, the water I give them will become in them a spring of water welling up to eternal life."

The woman said to him, "Sir, give me this water so that I won't get thirsty and have to keep coming here to draw water."

He told her, "Go, call your husband and come back."

Day 8: *"Will you give me a drink?" John 4:7*

"I have no husband," she replied.

Jesus said to her, "You are right when you say you have no husband. The fact is, you have had five husbands, and the man you now have is not your husband. What you have just said is quite true."

"Sir," the woman said, "I can see that you are a prophet. Our ancestors worshiped on this mountain, but you Jews claim that the place where we must worship is in Jerusalem."

"Woman," Jesus replied, "believe me, a time is coming when you will worship the Father neither on this mountain nor in Jerusalem. You Samaritans worship what you do not know; we worship what we do know, for salvation is from the Jews. Yet a time is coming and has now come when the true worshipers will worship the Father in the Spirit and in truth. . . ."

The woman said, "I know that Messiah" (called Christ) "is coming. When he comes, he will explain everything to us."

Then Jesus declared, "I, the one speaking to you—I am he."

JOHN 4:7-26

ALL OTHER PASSIONS LEAVE YOU PARCHED.
You thirst for comfort, for thrill, for novelty, for true liberty, for beauty, for wholeness, for shalom. But the five other lovers, the ten other passions, the one thousand other interests—all the lesser loves—leave you longing for more.

Our soul well knows this woman at the well.

You can actually feel that aching endlessness of thirst—that quiet longing for a fountain that undoes every sadness you've ever known, that aching for waters that quench a million dry and cracked prayers, that thirst to swallow down what will finally leave you wholly fulfilled. You know the desire to be ultimately quenched in every sense, never to thirst again.

And yet who can testify?

Your thirst for the realest life can drive you to drink all kinds of poisons that wreck your only life. "The Christian says, 'Creatures are not born with desires unless satisfaction for those desires exists,'" writes C. S. Lewis. "A baby feels hunger: well, there is such a thing as food. A duckling wants to swim: well, there is such a thing as water. Men feel sexual desire: well, there is such a thing as sex. If I find in myself a desire which no experience in this world can satisfy, the most probable explanation is that I was made for another world. If none of my earthly pleasures satisfy it, that does not prove that the universe is a fraud. Probably earthly pleasures were never meant to satisfy it, but only to arouse it, to suggest the real thing. If that is so, I must take care, on the one hand, never to despise, or be unthankful for, these earthly blessings, and on the other, never to mistake them for the something else of which they are only a kind of copy, or echo, or mirage. I must keep alive in myself the desire for my true country, which I shall not find till after death . . . I must make it the main object of life to press on to that other country and to help others to do the same."[1]

Everything you're looking for, hungry for, parched for, thirsty for, you can taste only when you drink divine Love down to your center.

All thirst is a thirst for love.

Unless the cavernous cravings of a soul are lowered into the well of His bottomless love, that soul will never be fulfilled, or fully well.

Who ever fully received all the love they craved from their father or mother, or any relationship ever? Because all the love we are looking for is found only in the inner chambers of Love Himself. What love but Love's alone is always enveloping, wholly accepting, deeply encompassing, perfectly responsive?

Your soul is never really parched for something but for Someone— Someone who will quench your thirst for all eternity. You're made for more than things of this earth; you're made for the *more* of glory, and even your worst doesn't disqualify you from being made for glory. This is the story that Jesus keeps whispering to you.

"If you knew the gift of God," Jesus said, looking her in the eye, "and who it is that is saying to you, 'Give me a drink,' you would have asked him, and he would have given you living water."

All there is to do is open your eyes, your mouth, your heart—this is not hard. (And, paradoxically, it may be the hardest of all.)

But really: You will not have to walk for water, you will not have to dig your own well, you will not have to keep filling broken cisterns that endlessly leak, you will not have to thirst. All is well, because the only well of genuine water is a lavish gift of God.

Swill down the relief of your saving and know Jesus speaks directly to the tender parts of you like He spoke directly to the ignored and belittled Samaritan woman. While some Pharisees on the street were called "the bruised Pharisees" because they preferred to close their eyes and bruise their knees walking into walls than to accidentally lay their eyes on any woman, Jesus was the Rabbi who looked this hurting woman in the eye.[2] Jesus was the Rabbi who looked at this bruised woman and broke down walls and said, "No one is too messed up to drink God's grace straight down."

Drink down the gift of God.

You do not have to earn the water, be good enough for the water, strive for the water, dig for the water, clamor to the front of any line, or be the best to get the water.

God's grace is simply a gift, not a medal.

God's grace is not about where you rank in life but about how you receive *His life*.

God's grace is not something you work to win but water you choose to simply drink. "Lord, give me this water that I may never be thirsty or have to keep coming here to some cheap well to draw water again and again," our prayer echoes hers.

God, in the person of Christ, who hung the stars, willingly hung on that cross and murmured the words, "My God, my God, why have you forsaken me?"—ancient words that He memorized and knew by heart from Psalm 22, and He knew reverberated in every human heart. And from those same parched and cracked lips, divine Love, the triune God Himself, panted, "I thirst." Not because the triune God needed earthly water, but because He felt how we're parched by any distance between our souls and our heavenly Father.

And pinned to that cross, He knew the rest of that same Psalm 22: "I am poured out like water. . . . My mouth is dried up like a potsherd, and my tongue sticks to the roof of my mouth; you lay me in the dust of death."

Jesus thirsted while He Himself was poured out like water on the cross, so every soul could drink of living water and never thirst for the rest of their lives: "To the thirsty I will give water without cost from the spring of the water of life" (Revelation 21:6).

Freely admit you're thirsty—and you freely get to drink. Your thirst is the only qualification you need to be quenched. "From Water-of-Life Well I give freely to the thirsty" (Revelation 21:6, MSG).

Your body, which holds your soul in this moment, is made of 60 percent water, with nearly three-fourths of brain and heart being composed of water; your lungs breathe in air that's more than 80 percent water; and even the strongest of your bones holding you up are nearly one-third water. Made of water, we crave water. And as the physical body needs water to live, the soul needs living water, or we're the living dead. Within our made-of-water body, our soul pants for true living water, or it dies of thirst. And because the soul needs spiritual water, and Christ is living water, then the way of Christ is never exclusionary, the way of Christ is ultimately necessary, because the soul literally dies without the only One who is living water.

Every other system of thought in the world claims to show you how to find the well of joy, but only Jesus says, "No, I am the living water springing from an ever-flowing well that will run the world over to find you."

Drink God or go dry. Nothing else will satisfy.

PERSONAL NOTES TO SOUL FROM TODAY'S PILGRIMAGE INTO THE HEART OF JESUS:

RUN TO THE WORD

After the two days he left for Galilee. (Now Jesus himself had pointed out that a prophet has no honor in his own country.) When he arrived in Galilee, the Galileans welcomed him. They had seen all that he had done in Jerusalem at the Passover Festival, for they also had been there.

Once more he visited Cana in Galilee, where he had turned the water into wine. And there was a certain royal official whose son lay sick at Capernaum. When this man heard that Jesus had arrived in Galilee from Judea, he went to him and begged him to come and heal his son, who was close to death.

"Unless you people see signs and wonders," Jesus told him, "you will never believe."

The royal official said, "Sir, come down before my child dies."

"Go," Jesus replied, "your son will live."

The man took Jesus at his word and departed. While he was still on the way, his servants met him with the news that his boy was living. When he inquired as to the time when his son got better, they said to him, "Yesterday, at one in the afternoon, the fever left him."

Then the father realized that this was the exact time at which Jesus had said to him, "Your son will live." So he and his whole household believed.

JOHN 4:43-53

Day 9: *"Sir, come . . ." John 4:49*

THERE'S A WORD that you can rest your whole life on, because He alone raises you to the realest, wholest life.

Isn't it a real and deep grief that we run to anything else that ultimately cannot satisfy or raise to life?

In the last, tortured, heaving moments of his boy's life, one royal official didn't stay to hold his son's hand, to hold his son's terrified eyes with comfort, to witness his boy's last breath—he turned to run a whole marathon of wild faith toward the only One who can ultimately save, the only One who is ultimately Life. Twenty-five panting miles, hour upon believing hour, his feet slapping the hard earth, driving his faith toward the only One he could ultimately trust.

When he finally flung himself at the feet of Jesus, his lungs on fire with a foolish run of faith, he begged, "Come."

Come before my son—*before my faith*—dies.

Pour out your heart to Jesus with expectation, and fully trust that Jesus will always move, but always in a way profoundly different from the way you'd expect.

Jesus didn't go to the boy.

Instead, He looked the begging father in the eye and gave him a word: "Go. Go, your son will live. Go, have faith in My words. Go, lean your life against My words and trust that they will hold."

We're desperate for Jesus to work the miracle, fix the problem, change the story, and raise our dead hopes—and Jesus comes as the Word, who raises us from the dead and changes our *life*. Do we dare to trust that the resurrection of hopes and life and dreams and all we deeply seek is actually found in the Word of God? And if we do, why not seek out His Word first thing?

Jesus' first miracle in Cana, instantaneously expediting the process of creating wine, was, in part, a miracle of time. But His second miracle in Cana, the healing of the son, was wholly a miracle of trust—the nobleman trusted that God's Word was enough and what he needed most. The father didn't take Jesus by the hand and lead Him back to his sick son—he simply took God at His Word.

Where you desperately want God to work a miracle, God says, "My Word comes to you and My Word always works a miracle *within you*."

You can think God is too far away to do His work—but God's Word is far more catalytic than you can fathom, and He works out His way, no matter what is in the way. You can think you somehow need God's visible presence to make any difference, but God's Word is His presence. His promise, His passion, His power, His Word makes the miraculous difference to all who keep coming to the living and active Word to find life. You already have the person of Christ with you, in person, when you live in the Word, when you live in Christ—*so you can fully live.*

We may seek signs and wonders, but God gives the Savior and the Word, and He wants us to seek Him, our sure Word, most.

In the long walk back to his son, the father was fueled by the promises of God with every step. Because the only way to bravely walk by faith, and not by sight, is to walk with His Word, breathe in His Word, dwell in His Word, lean on His Word, abide in His Word, meditate on His Word, so you do nothing less than take God at His Word.

What God surely speaks is what God surely does.

The whole of his pilgrimage, every long step of faith back to his son, the royal official dared to trust. The Word of God does more than affect your feelings about life; the Word of God effects radical change in your life.

Taking God at His Word is all the faith it takes to change your world. Why let anything take your attention, take your love away from a Word like that?

Whatever road you find yourself on, your walk of faith is paved with His rock-solid promises: He will never leave you or abandon you (Hebrews 13:5); He will never let you be separated from His love (Romans 8:31-39); He will refresh your life with His love (Zephaniah 3:17).

Whatever your road, your reality is that Love is always coming to meet you. Just as the royal official looked up to see breathlessly excited servants coming to meet him. *The son lives!*

The moment God's Word broke into the world, it broke all doubt and became reality, and the boy's fever broke.

What God surely speaks is what God surely does.

Though we may not know how God is working, this is what we can always know: All God's ways are working out Love. It's the unconditional love of God toward us that makes all conditions around us possible. And though the sickness of his son broke the father's heart, it caused him to run to Christ, which ultimately caused the saving of his whole household and the healing of all their hearts. This is no small thing; this is everything. Profound physical sickness can still, somehow, lead to profound soul healing. Great desperation can be the greatest gift, and we can find ourselves far more indebted to desperate times than we could ever realize. Because too often, we only turn our heart's cravings to God when all else leaves us craving more.

Real desperation can drive us into Christ's very real consolation.

This is one of the tenderly strange and loving paradoxes of the universe: Jesus works through affliction to bring an antidote for much that ails the soul.

It's when our hurting hearts tenderly break that the scales on our eyes can break and we can clearly see how we had strong faith all along—*but perhaps in all the wrong things*. It can turn out that we had more faith in strong hands and broad backs and good health and good news and a good word from good people and an extra dose of all kinds of great self-sufficiency than in God's Word and God's goodness. Affliction can reveal that we had more faith in approval and appearances and advantages than in God and His Word.

This is the way to not lose our way: Lose your faith in all things that are false gods, but don't lose your faith in the loving, kind ways of God. Have less faith in your limited point of view and more faith in the Word Himself, who has the whole and eternal perspective.

You can trust in the marrow of your bones: The God whose eye is on the sparrow will see to eternally reversing your every deep sorrow.

Which is why you can run your pilgrimage of faith with wild trust in the Word of God.

The exact Word of God exacts real change in the world, which is why we're called to be in the Word: *so it can effectively change us.*

And love us back to the realest life.

PERSONAL NOTES TO SOUL FROM TODAY'S PILGRIMAGE INTO THE HEART OF JESUS:

MADE WHOLE

Now in Jerusalem by the Sheep Gate there is a pool, called in Hebrew Beth-zatha, which has five porticoes. In these lay many invalids—blind, lame, and paralyzed. One man was there who had been ill for thirty-eight years. When Jesus saw him lying there and knew that he had been there a long time, he said to him, "Do you want to be made well?" The sick man answered him, "Sir, I have no one to put me into the pool when the water is stirred up; and while I am making my way, someone else steps down ahead of me." Jesus said to him, "Stand up, take your mat and walk." At once the man was made well, and he took up his mat and began to walk.

Now that day was a sabbath. So the Jews said to the man who had been cured, "It is the sabbath; it is not lawful for you to carry your mat." But he answered them, "The man who made me well said to me, 'Take up your mat and walk.'" They asked him, "Who is the man who said to you, 'Take it up and walk'?" Now the man who had been healed did not know who it was, for Jesus had disappeared in the crowd that was there. Later Jesus found him in the temple and said to him, "See, you have been made well! Do not sin any more."

JOHN 5:2-14, NRSV

Day *10*: *"Do you want to be made well?" John 5:6*

YOU CAN WAIT your whole life for your troubled waters and real wounds to be grazed by angel wings and to, at last, be made whole.

It was the time of feasting, the time of Passover, the time when the people of God remembered when the Lamb of God, the suffering love of God, the passion of God, covered them with His sacrifice so the angel of death would pass over them. And it was that same time of year when the hurting gathered, piling deep around the edges of the dark pool of Bethsaida, near the Sheep Gate, all seeking a heavenly ripple on waters and instantaneous healing.

One man had been waiting a lifetime for wholeness—more than a quarter of a century, thirty-eight long, aching years of hoping.

Sometimes faith is a long hoping in the right direction.

And now the Lamb of God, who has come straight down from heaven, stood in their midst, seeking their needing eyes, their longing faces.

Yet, although they were seeking healing, they didn't recognize their real Healer: "A blindness had come over these people at the pool; there they were, and there was Christ, who could heal them, but not a single one of them sought him. Their eyes were fixed on the water, expecting it to be troubled; they were so taken up with their own chosen way that the true way was neglected."[1]

It's a tender question for the aching soul: Why keep waiting for what we want to happen, why keep waiting for the miracle we've already birthed in our minds, why keep waiting for lightning to jolt from the heavens and part the impossible in just the way we imagined, why keep waiting for a word, instead of taking Him at His word, instead of keeping our hearts and minds on the Way Himself, who makes everything else happen?

Why keep looking for the way we want instead of looking toward the Way, who wants us?

Why keep waiting on false hopes and gimmicky shams and quick sells that never satisfy? Who longs to be made whole more than wanting the cheap thrills of steamy scenes or glittery screens or society status or any safe status quo?

It's a tender truth for the hurting soul: Sometimes we wait and want for so long that waiting and wanting become our identity instead of being well and whole, here and now.

It's why Jesus looks you in the eye and asks, "Do you want to be made well?"

The only way to wholeness is to wholly want the way of the Healer.

It's a tender guide who whispers to the tired soul: If you really want to be made well, you need to go to the right well.

Like the water in the purification pots at the wedding of Cana could not, in and of themselves, be made into the wine of the new Kingdom without being touched by the Lamb, so no stirred waters at the pool by the Sheep Gate, or any self-help gurus with imaginary angel wings, can ever make any soul whole without an actual encounter with Love Himself.

But the man at the pool almost missed Him.

Does Jesus ask us if we really want to be made well because, like the man who didn't move when the waters of the pool stirred with rippling possibility, we too have no imagination for being chosen?

Jesus' eyes find all the waiting, hurting ones, the ones struggling to believe in their chosenness.

Jesus' eyes find yours.

Jesus doesn't merely give you the reason He chooses you—He simply gives you Himself to *prove* how He chooses you.

You didn't earn being chosen, and your chosenness doesn't have to make sense, because Love Himself needs no human logic. God is Love and God is the logos, the logic of the world. He loves you not because of anything you've done but because Love is who He is, and He simply and wholly chooses to love you because He *chooses* to completely love you.

Yet the words that slip out of the man of infirmity are our words—the collective, haunted ache of all humanity: "Sir, I have no one . . ."

Are there sadder words than "I don't really have anyone—not really"? From our first breath, all we've ever wanted is a face looking into ours, searching ours, finding ours, delighting in ours. Since we first became a person on this planet, what we've wanted most is a person who wants us. When you rest on a face resting on yours, your soul rests, knowing you aren't alone and can now face anything.

And the face of Jesus gazes into your eyes and all your aching wanting, and He never turns away. "I will counsel you with my loving eye on you," comforts our triune God (Psalm 32:8).

We are all just wanting someone to be our person—and the Person of God has always wanted to be with us just as we are. "Look to the LORD and his strength; seek his face always" (Psalm 105:4). "As for me, I will be vindicated and will see your face; when I awake, I will be satisfied with seeing your likeness" (Psalm 17:15).

The fulfillment we seek is found only when we look full into His loving face. And it's only when we look into His face that we see there are more ways to wholeness than we've ever imagined, because we're looking into the eyes of the One who is the Way of wholeness Himself.

It can feel impossible to imagine being chosen by God, being passionately loved by God, being healed and whole through a very real and tender touch of God. It can be easier to do "what almost all of us are wont to do; for he limits the assistance of God according to his own thought, and does not venture to promise to himself any thing more than he conceives in his mind," writes John Calvin.[2]

How could any of the limited number of ways we conceive for good ever compare to all the healing ways of the One who conceived us and is working good through all the universe?

It's a tender epiphany for the honest soul: Sometimes our worst illness is our shriveled imagination for all the ways God loves us enough to work wellness and wholeness into the depths of our souls.

Sometimes the most important question to ask our waiting souls is simply *What if you only got the way you wanted but missed the better ways God wanted?*

"Rise, take up your bed and walk," Jesus said, nodding toward everyone stuck in paralysis.

Jesus told the one stuck in paralysis to do what he'd *never* done. For thirty-eight years, the man hadn't once risen, hadn't once simply carried what he'd always relied upon, hadn't once really walked forward.

This is always the way: Take the next step in the way of obedience, take the next step on your pilgrimage, and the way to wholeness begins to become clear.

And the Word of God does all the real work within you as you obey and trust that though you may not yet see how God is working, the Way is working everything out. Even though you may not yet see what has changed, you can act on Jesus' Word, trust in Jesus' Word, lean on Jesus' Word: "At once the man was made well, and he took up his mat and began to walk."

The best way to find the way through is to keep walking the way of obedience. This is the pilgrimage of our lives.

Jesus takes your hand and whispers, close and tender, "See, you have been made well! Do not sin anymore . . ."

And we nod, our eyes not leaving His.

His heart beating whole and well within us.

PERSONAL NOTES TO SOUL FROM TODAY'S PILGRIMAGE INTO THE HEART OF JESUS:

BOUNTY

After this Jesus went away to the other side of the Sea of Galilee, which is the Sea of Tiberias. And a large crowd was following him, because they saw the signs that he was doing on the sick. Jesus went up on the mountain, and there he sat down with his disciples. Now the Passover, the feast of the Jews, was at hand. Lifting up his eyes, then, and seeing that a large crowd was coming toward him, Jesus said to Philip, "Where are we to buy bread, so that these people may eat?" He said this to test him, for he himself knew what he would do. Philip answered him, "Two hundred denarii worth of bread would not be enough for each of them to get a little." One of his disciples, Andrew, Simon Peter's brother, said to him, "There is a boy here who has five barley loaves and two fish, but what are they for so many?"

Jesus said, "Have the people sit down." Now there was much grass in the place. So the men sat down, about five thousand in number. Jesus then took the loaves, and when he had given thanks, he distributed them to those who were seated. So also the fish, as much as they wanted. And when they had eaten their fill, he told his disciples, "Gather up the leftover fragments, that nothing may be lost." So they gathered them up and filled twelve baskets with fragments from the five barley loaves left by those who had eaten.

When the people saw the sign he had done, they said, "This is indeed the Prophet who is to come into the world!"

JOHN 6:1-14, ESV

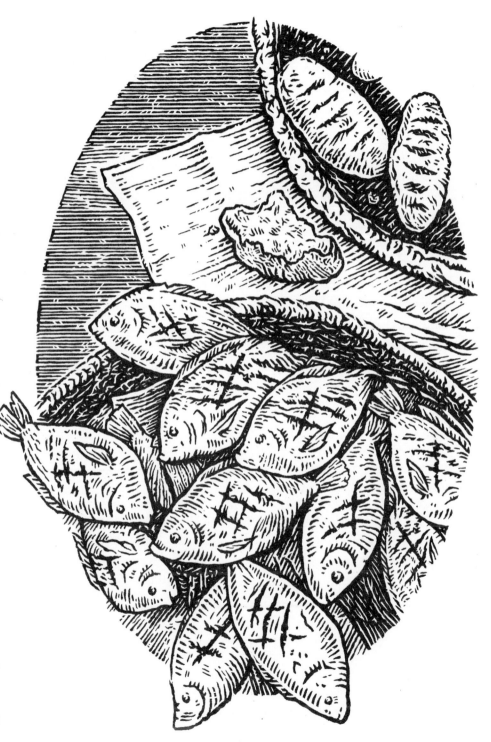

Day *11: "Gather up the leftover fragments, that nothing may be lost." John 6:12*

YOU AREN'T ALONE.

We're all looking for signs that we're loved, and we are with every single one of the five thousand, who, whether they knew it or not, had all come looking for a sign that they were loved. Is the sign and wonder we're all really looking for the same: that we're loved by the One who is Love?

In Greek, the Word gives the sense that "the multitude 'kept following' Jesus because they 'continually saw' the signs that He 'habitually did' for the sick."[1] Yet if God doesn't keep giving us signs, keep giving us our own way, is it possible we will no longer keep following Him wholeheartedly but instead meander off the Way, thinking we know a better way into the realest life?

Is it possible to follow Jesus looking for signs of all kinds of healing, when what actually heals us is looking to Him who is always looking at us with the kindest love, bearing scars that heal ours?

In His compassion, Love Himself looks into our eyes, and He knows what it is to be one of us, to hurt like us, to face all kinds of enemies like we do, to be a sheep like us. And He has mercy on us because we are "like a sheep without a shepherd" (Mark 6:34). So He shepherds your soul close with the Word, consoles your wounds with wisdom, nourishes your soul-cravings with Himself.

You can feel the crush of people. Five thousand men—more than twenty thousand people, including women and children—had followed Jesus up the steep terrain overlooking the lapping waters of Lake Galilee from the east. When Jesus, who had been feeding the people with His Words, asked His disciples what it might look like to feed all those people, Philip answered that eight whole months of work and wages wouldn't give every mouth even one bite of bread.

You know how Philip-thinking still happens now: You can live your life thinking in terms of either earthly resources or divine resources. There is a whole world of difference between thinking in the practical and thinking in the miraculous—which ultimately leads you to two very different places. And hadn't Philip himself witnessed with his own two eyes how divine Love worked miracles, speaking sinews into strength, enlivening veins through His voice alone, unfolding bodies into wholeness through His words?

But seeing miracles with your own eyes doesn't stop filmy cataracts from growing over the eyes of your heart.

Who hasn't seen the miraculous images of our own blue marble of Earth spinning safe across space, felt the miracle under your very own hand of the sure and steady thrum of life pulsing through your veins, or held the miracle of a whole, fresh new human being in your arms—love made life? (Love always makes life.) And yet who hasn't pulled some Philip-thinking in the blink of an eye and flipped from faithing to doubting?

But gazing long into His face can burn off the scales of our soul-cataracts. It's the realest story you'll ever gaze upon: Bread being bread, God giving God, Love lavishing love, loving us to life.

Every pupil of Jesus needs eyes that see through a lens of faith, and devout disciples always see the possibility of divine resources.

One poor little boy with his poor little loaves—in a crowd of twenty thousand hungry people—looked to Jesus and gave what little he had. When you give what you have to Jesus, you should know this: Losing terrifies, surrender terrifies, not having control terrifies. But Jesus takes. And Jesus remakes. You can feel the relief of it, too: The one who gives up control to Christ is given more comfort in Christ.

And Jesus draws close: "My people will be filled with my bounty" (Jeremiah 31:14).

You can feel His fulfilling presence. You know a Love who makes even the meager into the most, who takes your poverty of possibility and makes it into a bounty of serenity.

"When [Jesus] had given thanks, he distributed them to those who were seated. So also the fish, as much as they wanted."

You can always have as much of God as you want.

And in the loving hands of God, little becomes lavishness and not enough becomes overabundance. And from much thanks, there comes more joy than imagined.

Giving thanks for very little preceded the miracle of more than enough grace.

Giving thanks always precedes the miracle of more than enough joy.

Lifting hands in thanks is the very real way you let go of all that's in your hands. Thanksgiving is how we *give things*—give much, give everything—to God.

And it doesn't matter how small anything is—what matters is whose large hands they are in. All that's in your hands—put it all into God's hands. Because what matters is that all matter, in His hands, becomes miraculous.

Letting go lets miracles begin.

In the end, in Christ, there will always be more than enough, even when it doesn't seem like there is enough to start with. First the dying, then the multiplying. The math of God is that, in Him, the broken and divided, the given and subtracted, equals multiplied abundance.

When John penned this miraculous love story several decades later, there were more than twenty thousand people who had actually been there who could have challenged this document circulating Palestine. They could have disputed it, dismissed it, squashed it before it ever left that small corner of the world. The only way John's love letter, detailing miracle after miracle, witnessed by thousands upon thousands, could have withstood peer review and spread across the world was that the miracles *actually happened*.

Christianity is not some concocted, imaginary, allegorical fantasy; Christianity is robustly rooted in accuracy, veracity, credibility, historicity, and reality.

Not only does your Love, your triune God, give you your daily manna, your daily bread, your daily ration—He gives you Himself. This is not fantasy; this is your reality.

The Love of your life is a greater Moses, through whom God provided manna for the multitudes in the desert. He is a greater Elisha, through whom God provided bread to the sons of the prophets. He is the greatest Word, who feeds souls that do not live by bread alone but are resuscitated by the warm breath of the words of His mouth.

And in the end, twelve baskets were filled to the brim with leftovers, the number twelve noted because the promise is that there will always be provision not only for each of the twelve tribes of Israel but for every one of God's adopted children.

Fear not: There will never be a time you will not get to feast on the sustaining strength of Him.

And though God can and does keep coming with new provisions, He still collects everything left over, like He collects every tear of your grief. Because God wastes nothing and keeps everything and redeems everything, because God keeps *you* always.

How many had come only because they had seen miraculous healings? How many had stayed only because they had eaten miraculous food but actually had no imagination that the ultimate miracle would be something more profound than political power? How many had yet to grasp that He came to break death's reign over their lives, to be in intimate communion with them now and for forever?

His love for you is the sign you've been looking for your whole life; His unwavering, unconditional love is the wonder you've really been on this pilgrimage looking for.

And the Cross marks you as being loved out of this world and into a taste of heaven, even right now, in this holy moment.

PERSONAL NOTES TO SOUL FROM TODAY'S PILGRIMAGE INTO THE HEART OF JESUS:

IN YOUR
STORMIEST
VORTEX

When evening came, his disciples went down to
the sea, got into a boat, and started across the sea
to Capernaum. It was now dark, and Jesus had not
yet come to them. The sea became rough because
a strong wind was blowing. When they had rowed
about three or four miles, they saw Jesus walking
on the sea and coming near the boat, and they were
frightened. But he said to them, "It is I; do not be
afraid." Then they were glad to take him into the
boat, and immediately the boat was at the land to
which they were going.

JOHN 6:16-21, ESV

Day *12*: *"It is I; do not be afraid." John 6:20*

IT'S OKAY TO WANT to get to the other side.

It's okay to want to get to the other side of this mountain range, the other side of this chapter, the other side of this struggle, the other side of this heartbreak.

It truly is okay. You want to be laughing and whole on the other side in all the ways you always dreamed your story would go.

But high waves smash relentlessly, and whipping winds sting. You're bone weary from endless rowing. And it turns out? You can have twelve baskets of leftover miracle food at your feet right there in your boat, right there in the midst of your storm—proof of the supernatural provision around you everywhere—and still have immeasurable fear in your heart.

Like those disciples, you feel it: eight hours of rowing toward Capernaum into straight-line winds, terrified and still only halfway across the lake. Life is waves, and the transformation of getting to the other side of anything will bring rising crests and crashing lows and grueling storms. This is always how the process goes. There is more than just accepting the process—there is accepting and trusting the ways of the One who rules the waves and the whole process.

You aren't ever alone in any of your waves.

There may be darkness on the face of the deep, and every face is looking for a face—and the face of Jesus is always turned toward ours.

No matter how high the waves, how dark the depths, how wild the wind or the storm, there is Jesus' face coming across the waves to be with you. Circumstances don't have to take a turn to turn back fear; simply an awareness of His presence alone can turn back fear.

You can trust, right here and now, in your storm, that you are in the presence of the supernatural, of the otherworldly, of the One whose heel walks on waves like a highway and looks you in the eye and says, "It is I"—the same holy gaze that set the bush ablaze for Moses with the reverberating "I Am."

God doesn't just exist. God *is* existence. God walks the waves because this is His world—this is our Father's world. The waves are under Him, and the storms are under Him, and the chaos and the struggle are under Him, and He takes us so we are soul-safe in Him.

As surely as you can readily say that you exist, that you can say, "I am," God meets your eye and says, "I exist. I Am. I Am here. It is I." God is here. It is *I*, our first Love, the great I Am who always says, "I Am here, right here. I Am over your storming vortex. I Am above this struggle. I Am all power, all rule, all Love, and I Am *all for you.*"

How can we not turn to Him and whisper back, "And here I am. Here is my storm, here is my ache, here are my waves, here are all my other loves. Here I am, take me. Loving You, living in You is my life's passion, my only passageway through."

No other love compares to this Love—who is our life.

All other loves are washed away in the waves. He is center. Jesus is God Almighty, with all authority, and either He is your center or He is nothing; there is no periphery. The only way to accept His Love is to accept His lordship. There's no walking on the fence with Jesus; there's only centering everything on Him so you can walk on water to follow Him—or staying in the seemingly calm water that will slowly boil you to death.

The only way to cross to the other side of anything is to trust that real calm isn't found in changing exterior circumstances but in an interior focus on the unchanging love of God. Calm isn't a function of circumstances; calm is a function of focusing on God. And His love is relentlessly doing holy interior work within us through these hard exterior circumstances. Our Love doesn't just want to make us feel good; He wants to make *us* good.

He will get you to the other side, and He will change you on the inside.

That's what storms are for: Storms transport, storms transform.

While we ache to be loved by Love Himself through this storm, we can yet fear His holy, passionate love in this storm because the heat of a love like this doesn't let us be in control, but refines us, sanctifies us, burns off the dross, reforges us, and reforms us. If you let Him in the boat, you may fear losing control to Him, but would you rather be lost at sea in a boat that can never get through to the other side of this? Because there's no real crossing to the other side unless the One who walks on water is by your side.

These conflicting pressure systems—craving His passionate love and yet passionately wanting our own way—can stir a storm within us that's far greater than any storm surrounding us.

The Word across all our waves comes and holds us:

It is I—
so why
fear anything?
I AM here—no fear.

The white heat of His passionate, purifying love is not something to fear but is the deepest comfort you can always draw near to through every storm.

Because it was His holy love for you that drove Him to the cross, where the iron nails drove through your name, written like a love note on His hand. Because at the Cross, He faced the fury and storm of your sin and went down into the depths of your death, but His holiness caused Him to conquer all the hellish chaos and rise, your name on His lips, like the love song He can't ever stop singing. And if you hide in His holiness, no storm can ever sink you now.

When you accept the passionate love of Jesus into your vessel, you don't row harder to get to the other side—you've already arrived, already been accepted there on the other side, into the paradise of His presence.

The miracle of arriving didn't happen until the disciples "were glad to take him into the boat." And the miracle doesn't happen until you willingly receive all the white-hot passion of Christ into your surrendered heart.

A soul no sooner takes the love of Christ to heart than it immediately arrives in the safest, deepest love that no storm can ever touch—in the arms of Love who carries you through to the other side.

The pilgrimage is always into the intimacy of His presence.

PERSONAL NOTES TO SOUL FROM TODAY'S PILGRIMAGE INTO THE HEART OF JESUS:

THE BREAD OF GOD

When they found him on the other side of the lake, they asked him, "Rabbi, when did you get here?"

Jesus answered, "Very truly I tell you, you are looking for me, not because you saw the signs I performed but because you ate the loaves and had your fill. Do not work for food that spoils, but for food that endures to eternal life, which the Son of Man will give you. For on him God the Father has placed his seal of approval."

Then they asked him, "What must we do to do the works God requires?"

Jesus answered, "The work of God is this: to believe in the one he has sent."

So they asked him, "What sign then will you give that we may see it and believe you? What will you do? Our ancestors ate the manna in the wilderness; as it is written: 'He gave them bread from heaven to eat.'"

Jesus said to them, "Very truly I tell you, it is not Moses who has given you the bread from heaven, but it is my Father who gives you the true bread from heaven. For the bread of God is the bread that comes down from heaven and gives life to the world."

"Sir," they said, "always give us this bread."

Then Jesus declared, "I am the bread of life. Whoever comes to me will never go hungry, and whoever believes in me will never be thirsty.

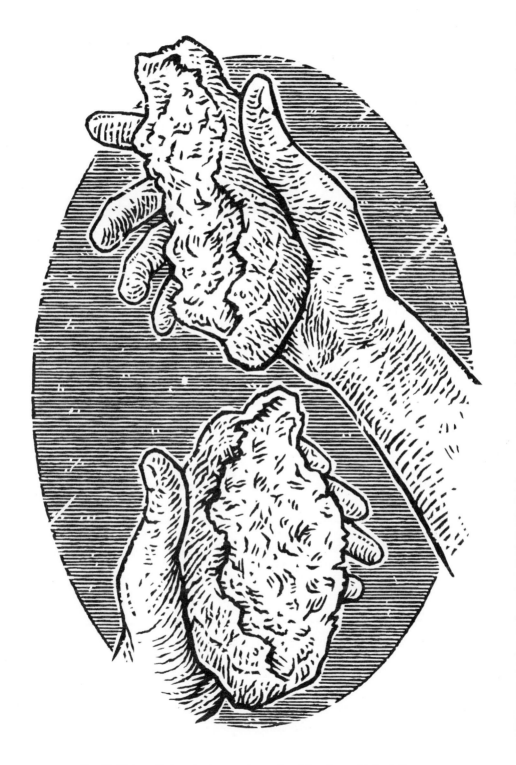

Day *13*: *"It is my Father who gives you the true bread from heaven." John 6:32*

But as I told you, you have seen me and still you do not believe. All those the Father gives me will come to me, and whoever comes to me I will never drive away. For I have come down from heaven not to do my will but to do the will of him who sent me. And this is the will of him who sent me, that I shall lose none of all those he has given me, but raise them up at the last day. For my Father's will is that everyone who looks to the Son and believes in him shall have eternal life, and I will raise them up at the last day."

At this the Jews there began to grumble about him because he said, "I am the bread that came down from heaven." They said, "Is this not Jesus, the son of Joseph, whose father and mother we know? How can he now say, 'I came down from heaven'?"

"Stop grumbling among yourselves," Jesus answered. "No one can come to me unless the Father who sent me draws them, and I will raise them up at the last day. It is written in the Prophets: 'They will all be taught by God.' Everyone who has heard the Father and learned from him comes to me. No one has seen the Father except the one who is from God; only he has seen the Father. Very truly I tell you, the one who believes has eternal life. I am the bread of life. Your ancestors ate the manna in the wilderness, yet they died. But here is the bread that comes down from heaven, which anyone may eat and not die. I am the living bread that came down from heaven. Whoever eats this bread will live forever. This bread is my flesh, which I will give for the life of the world."

JOHN 6:25-51

ISN'T IT A MIRACLE that you got swept up in this pressing crowd that keeps following Jesus?

It's because you are being drawn by God. Right now, as you are looking at this page, you are looking for Jesus, who, right now, is looking for you.

But is it possible that Jesus turns to find us in the crowd and says to us, "Very truly I tell you, you are looking for Me, not because you saw the signs I performed but because you ate the loaves and had your fill."

Is there a part of us that's starving after a miracle worker, rather than trusting the work of our Maker?

Is there a part of us with materialistic notions about the Kingdom of God, or are we truly focused on the Messiah?

Through the crowd, Jesus finds our eyes and speaks steadiness to the deepest parts of our souls: "I am the bread of life. Whoever comes to me will never go hungry, and whoever believes in me will never be thirsty."

What you have an appetite for is what you are actually most ardent about.

Jesus' definition of genuine Christians is those who are hungry for the white-hot heat of His heart instead of those who stuff themselves with the bland, unfulfilling, reheated substitutes of this world.

Because the reality is, if you have little appetite for God, it may be because you've filled yourself up on the empty calories of this world's all-you-can-eat buffet. Steal nibbles of the cheap sweets of this world long enough, and you ruin your appetite for God. When we aren't hungry for God, is that a sign that we've feasted for too long on the fluff of this world?

You are what you consume.

The news, the screens, the conversations, the desires—every passion that consumes you becomes you.

It's tender to sit with: Eat dead things, and you live a dead life.

Because the reality is: All that is grown from the dust of this earth is the food of the dead. "For one who thinks food in itself is the source of life, eating is communion with the dying world, it is communion with death. Food itself is dead, it is life that has died and it must be kept in refrigerators like a corpse," writes theologian Alexander Schmemann.[1] There is only one living source of sustenance in all the world, because He alone comes from beyond the walls of this world—the One who says, "I Am living bread. I Am living water."

Any nourishment apart from the Bread of Life eventually goes bad. The only soul food that never spoils is found in our Savior. And the way to endure to eternal life is to keep eating "food that endures to eternal life." It's surreal joy to sit with: *Eat living bread, and you live forever!*

Consume the passion of God, the Bread who is Jesus, and you become like the love of Christ—you become a "little Christ." *You finally become fully alive!*

His suffering love is meant to be savored, swallowed down—His strength into your sinews. His kind of supernatural love you have to get into your soul, pulsing through your veins, enlarging the chambers of your heart, enlivening the neural matter of your mind, surging and invigorating and beating out the exhilarating rhythm of your being, the essence of you—*becoming* you.

This kind of passionate vitality is real Christianity!

The Bread of Life is the *Person* of Jesus. Linger with His friendship. He is Lord and Lover, for better or worse, not some lackey who'd better deliver for us or else. Be held in His intimacy. Taste His Communion. This Bread of God does not require us to have a degree or pedigree to eat of His sweetness. Let the little children come, let anyone come—anyone can simply come and eat bread. Who wants to live?

"This bread is my flesh, which I will give for the life of the world," Jesus said, stretching out His hand toward you (John 6:51).

His body: for the life of the world.

His heart: loving the world to life.

The presence of God is the only sustenance that actually sustains a soul. The ultimate love feast is God.

The passion of God for you isn't a love you can merely reflect on, think about, neatly consider—a cerebral exercise in hypothesis. The passion of God is a love meant to be metabolized. Divine love begs to be digested.

The meal you never stop hungering for is the mind and heart of God. And your broken heart gets to feel the deepest comfort: He who is the Bread of Life is broken bread for you. Because He knows that a loaf still whole leaves you wholly wanting. Only a piece of broken bread can fill you. Jesus knows your brokenness, and He knows that your brokenness can only know wholeness if He goes to the Cross and, like bread, is broken and given for you. If Jesus were only perfection, you would only feel condemnation. But because Jesus is perfection who became broken for all your brokenness, your broken heart can experience wholeness.

Jesus cups your broken heart, your starved soul, your parched passions, looks you in the eye and whispers, "This bread is my flesh, which I will give for the life of the world."

You get loved to life! All your dead and broken places can be healed, fulfilled, revived, and made wholly alive.

The only way to taste this Bread of heaven is to know that you don't work for it; you simply open your heart wide to receive the gift of it.

The work of God in you is not hard work, or more work, or good works, or better works. The work of God in you is simply the work of faithing in Him, leaning on Him, trusting in Him, not wavering in your allegiance to Him, savoring the taste of His Love *more than any other love in your life.*

The God who buys out all the liens on your life with His own sacrificed heart is worthy of leaning the whole of your heart on.

The work God calls you to is to taste and trust Him when you don't know how to.

This is your real daily pilgrimage: Your life's real work is to trust that God is really working.

Slowly taste the Bread of God and trust, even when you can't see, how the Bread is working within—for your life in the world, for the love of the world.

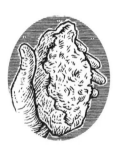

PERSONAL NOTES TO SOUL FROM TODAY'S PILGRIMAGE INTO THE HEART OF JESUS:

WHERE CAN YOU GO?

On hearing it, many of his disciples said, "This is a hard teaching. Who can accept it?"

Aware that his disciples were grumbling about this, Jesus said to them, "Does this offend you? Then what if you see the Son of Man ascend to where he was before! The Spirit gives life; the flesh counts for nothing. The words I have spoken to you—they are full of the Spirit and life. Yet there are some of you who do not believe." For Jesus had known from the beginning which of them did not believe and who would betray him. He went on to say, "This is why I told you that no one can come to me unless the Father has enabled them."

From this time many of his disciples turned back and no longer followed him.

"You do not want to leave too, do you?" Jesus asked the Twelve.

Simon Peter answered him, "Lord, to whom shall we go? You have the words of eternal life. We have come to believe and to know that you are the Holy One of God."

Then Jesus replied, "Have I not chosen you, the Twelve? Yet one of you is a devil!" (He meant Judas, the son of Simon Iscariot, who, though one of the Twelve, was later to betray him.)

JOHN 6:60-71

Day 14: "Lord, to whom shall we go?" John 6:68

YOU MAY SEE JESUS' hand stretched out to you, because He means to touch your heart, that His words impress, reshape, reform, remake you, so you can actually fully know Him.

Who can accept it?

The passion of God is freely given—*and may cost you everything.*

It can be a hard teaching to eat the words of Christ. It is a hard teaching to turn over your interior tables so you can turn and enter the Temple of His love. It is a hard teaching to take the cup and nod when you receive the instruction "Do whatever He tells you." It is a hard teaching to eat His Word, savor Him as your only Bread. But there are hard teachings that are the softest place in all the world to land.

Who can accept Him?

These realities of the universe are not so much hard to understand as they are hard to stand and accept and swallow down as grace, as reviving love.

You are truly following Jesus when you keep hungering for Him, swallowing His Word, savoring His love, so you slowly become like Him.

In the midst of a world with a million other words, Jesus' followers echo the words of God's prophets: "When your words came, I ate them; they were my joy and my heart's delight" (Jeremiah 15:16). The sweetest comfort food in all the world is the Word. Delight in every line, the sweet sustenance your soul craves.

It can be tender and hard for a heart to accept: The actual meat and drink of your life is whatever you can't do without, day in and out. *You are what you consume.*

Jesus' eyes search your heart and whisper to you there next to the woman at the well, next to the sellers at the tables in the Temple, in front of the man at the pool waters waiting for angel wings, and behind the running Roman official with the deathly sick son. And He asks you, "Am I your bread and drink? Am I what you crave to taste and hunger to swallow? Am I who you have an insatiable appetite for? Do you lean on Me to give you strength to stand? Am I your fuel, am I your center, am I your very life? Am I your one love, your greatest passion?"

It can be easy to follow God as long as He's following your terms. But anyone who follows Christ on their own terms, for a return on investment, misses out on intimate communion with the God of the universe and is instead left holding a detailed contract with a business acquaintance. Who can examine if they're just checking off a to-do list with God, for a payback of miracles? Christianity is never about whether it pays to follow Jesus, because Jesus already paid for your every wrong with His back on the cross. Christianity is about following Jesus to get the riches of Jesus Himself.

When you truly believe that Jesus has the words of life, you believe there is a tender world of difference between a relationship with God that is merely transactional and one that is wholly covenantal. There is a holy world of difference between a relationship with God that embraces and enters into suffering, knowing that suffering is always exactly the shape and form and heart of His passion, and the kind of relationship that braces to avoid all suffering, passionately demanding a life of no suffering if God really loves us.

"You do not want to leave too, do you?" The gentle heart of Jesus searches the tender heart of every one of His followers. If God asks much of you, how much will you answer with your life? If God asks for complete authority over your life but doesn't give you completely what you want, do you still completely give yourself to Him?

The passionate love of God is never fully experienced on our transactional terms but only in His covenantal arms. Followers of Jesus passionately follow Jesus to fully experience the passion of Jesus. Full stop.

This is a tender epiphany that hard roads can give you: You always get to decide if the hard teachings of Jesus drive you away from Jesus or drive you into the arms of Jesus, to live the way of Jesus. "Christ will detain none with him against their wills; his soldiers are volunteers, not pressed men," writes Matthew Henry.[1]

Our hearts ponder the power of Jesus' question, and we answer with Peter: "Lord, to whom shall we go? You have the words of eternal life."

Where can we go when there are days coming in our story far harder than any we could imagine, when there are shock calls, when there's devastating, disorienting news that rips the air from the lungs, when there are ugly graves and hard funerals for every one of us who has ever loved, because love and loss live with each other? Where in this hurting world can you go?

Honestly, where is there real comfort in all the cosmos if you forsake the consolation of Christ?

How could any of the husks of this world be a safe haven for your only soul or feed the empty places within? Every earthly love will eventually fail, every worldly foundation will eventually crack, and every feast this old world can muster isn't a rich enough portion for your only soul. *So where is a soul to go?*

This is a world of story, of hard stories, of hearts dying in a thousand painful ways, of a million cheap and lying stories warring against one another in a battle for souls, leaving countless souls as the walking dead. And there is only one story in all the world that has the words of eternal life. Only one story is a story full of Spirit, only one story is a story full of soul-manna, only one story is a love story that slays time and sin and woos souls for all of forever.

Honestly, to whom shall you go but to the only One who can give you a new heart and a new Spirit? What else could ever attract and draw hearts like that? To whom shall you go but to the only One who has loved you to death and back to the realest life, to the only One whose passion has saved you so your every real crisis is now really over and you are soul-safe for forever now?

A love like His deeply binds us to Him, which is what deeply binds our broken hearts into more wholeness.

All roads don't lead to Rome—there is one road, and one road only, that leads to real hope, and His name is Jesus.

Life is brutally hard. And the only way to have what you need to rise to all the hard is to metabolize all Christ's strengthening, otherworldly, hard teachings, and be filled with Christ Himself.

Because it turns out in the end: The way to know you are following Jesus is that you aren't going anywhere else to find a way through your life.

Every genuine pilgrim lives with the only real compass in the cosmos—Christ.

This is the only pilgrimage worthy of your time, your life. There is nowhere for us in the universe to go but to God alone.

PERSONAL NOTES TO SOUL FROM TODAY'S PILGRIMAGE INTO THE HEART OF JESUS:

NOT CONDEMNED

Jesus went to the Mount of Olives. At dawn he appeared again in the temple courts, where all the people gathered around him, and he sat down to teach them. The teachers of the law and the Pharisees brought in a woman caught in adultery. They made her stand before the group and said to Jesus, "Teacher, this woman was caught in the act of adultery. In the Law Moses commanded us to stone such women. Now what do you say?" They were using this question as a trap, in order to have a basis for accusing him.

But Jesus bent down and started to write on the ground with his finger. When they kept on questioning him, he straightened up and said to them, "Let any one of you who is without sin be the first to throw a stone at her." Again he stooped down and wrote on the ground.

At this, those who heard began to go away one at a time, the older ones first, until only Jesus was left, with the woman still standing there. Jesus straightened up and asked her, "Woman, where are they? Has no one condemned you?"

"No one, sir," she said.

"Then neither do I condemn you," Jesus declared. "Go now and leave your life of sin."

JOHN 8:1-11

Day 15: *"Neither do I condemn you." John 8:11*

It reverberates off the walls of the deepest pits, straight across the universe, from the very throne room of God's heart, quaking your heart awake.

You are not condemned, though you are guilty of the hidden thing, the unspoken thing, the proud thing, the gossiping thing, the thing you keep doing again and again, the thing you would do anything to take back and get a do-over for, the thing about you that you'd never want shared at any dinner table, from any microphone, or in any headline. You are not condemned, even though there are people you ended up failing. Even though there are wounds you've caused and damage you've done but didn't intend. Even though there are all those things you desperately wish you could undo.

"Therefore, there is now no condemnation for those who are in Christ Jesus" (Romans 8:1), because the love of your life, Jesus, takes all the condemnation on Himself.

These seven words, "You are guilty, but you aren't condemned"—this is the perfection of the gospel. Write them up the walls of your cerebrum, across your forehead so you see them in every mirror you'll ever look into.

What the woman wrapped in bedsheets didn't know was that the Pharisees and teachers of the law were about to trap her—the woman ensnared and caught in adultery.

To accuse anyone of adultery, the bar was such that there could be absolutely no presumption or innuendo or question; one had to be caught in the physical act. Yet it was on her alone that the trap snapped shut, not the man tangled in the sheets. She alone was dragged out of bed and publicly humiliated, swathed in a tangle of shame—that very verb *caught* in the original Greek indicating "taken with her shame upon her."[1] Shame swells in isolation, grows larger and larger when it lives alone. And when shame is upon you, you can't remember how His grace could ever be upon you, how grace is always coming to meet you, how grace never wants to leave you. Shame hungrily devours any hope you can change, while grace keeps laying out a feast of hope and says, "Come, eat."

When this woman was flung in front of God in the flesh, the Word said nothing but bent down in the dust like He did at our Eden beginning, when He kissed us to life out of dust. And with the same finger that carved stars out of nothing, there, in the dirt, the Word wrote words—the only time Jesus is ever recorded writing.

"In the story of the woman taken in adultery we are told Christ bent down and scribbled in the dust with His finger," writes C. S. Lewis. "Nothing comes of this. No one has ever based any doctrine on it. And the art of inventing little irrelevant details to make an imaginary scene more convincing is a purely modern art. Surely the only explanation of this passage is that the thing really happened? The author put it in simply because he had *seen* it."[2] Who knows what Jesus wrote in the dust, but what we know is that this happened, that there were eyewitnesses who saw the fingers that handmade the heavens etching words in the dirt of this earth.

Is it possible that Jesus scrawled across the granules the sins committed by her accusers? Were her accusers cut to the quick with all their own sins as His fingers cut through the dust?

"Throw a stone," Jesus said, straightening up. "Just make sure that whoever throws that stone hasn't ever done anything worthy of having a stone cast at him."

Hasn't it been true across all the ages? The heart always enlarges the sins in another heart while shrinking the sin in its own.

Without another word, the Word knelt and scrawled more in the sand. And one by one, the woman's accusers fell away, dominoes of pride and power knocked down.

The woman looked around. The woman looked down. The tender face of Jesus, His compassionate eyes searching hers, was below her.

The God of the heavens has lowered Himself to be the floor of love under your shame, the sureness of love under your humiliation, the love that goes lower than your most devastating low.

Wherever we find ourselves, God goes lower to be the lifter of our chins, the catcher of our tears, the loving arms underneath us, holding us and carrying us through.

Jesus holds your story in gentle hands because He never stops holding your need for gentleness at the center of His awareness.

He holds our eyes, holds our chin, and whispers, "Neither do I condemn you . . ." because He will take all your condemnation.

The stones that should be cast at you—He takes them.

The arrows that should be turned on you—He takes them.

The shame, the humiliation, the guilt—He takes them all. Because He takes all of you.

Behold, the Lamb of God, who takes away the sins of the world—so He can take you and love you to life.

He is your rescue, your shield, your Lamb, your love forever-sealed. He kisses you with grace and says, "Go now and leave your life of sin."

Go, and sin no more.

Entering into the depths of His love is how you leave behind a life of sin.

What turns the human heart around is not shame, not guilt, not anger, not accusations, not bigger bootstraps, not some self-help plan; what turns the human heart around is simply what the human heart is made for: *love.*

Jesus knows it is perfect love that casts out fear, perfect love that casts out cravings, perfect love that casts out hang-ups, perfect love that casts out sin.

This is the way of the life-giving love of God: Jesus completely embraced people before they completely embraced changing.

The way of Jesus is to scandalously love people before they change their scandalous ways.

The pilgrimage into a new way of being begins with just finding ways to keep looking into His eyes.

PERSONAL NOTES TO SOUL FROM TODAY'S PILGRIMAGE INTO THE HEART OF JESUS:

_____

_____

_____

_____

WHEREVER

WE FIND

OURSELVES,

GOD GOES

LOWER TO BE

THE LIFTER

OF OUR CHINS.

LIGHT HAS DAWNED

When Jesus spoke again to the people, he said, "I am the light of the world. Whoever follows me will never walk in darkness, but will have the light of life."

The Pharisees challenged him, "Here you are, appearing as your own witness; your testimony is not valid."

Jesus answered, "Even if I testify on my own behalf, my testimony is valid, for I know where I came from and where I am going. But you have no idea where I come from or where I am going. You judge by human standards; I pass judgment on no one. But if I do judge, my decisions are true, because I am not alone. I stand with the Father, who sent me. In your own Law it is written that the testimony of two witnesses is true. I am one who testifies for myself; my other witness is the Father, who sent me."

Then they asked him, "Where is your father?"

"You do not know me or my Father," Jesus replied. "If you knew me, you would know my Father also."

JOHN 8:12-19

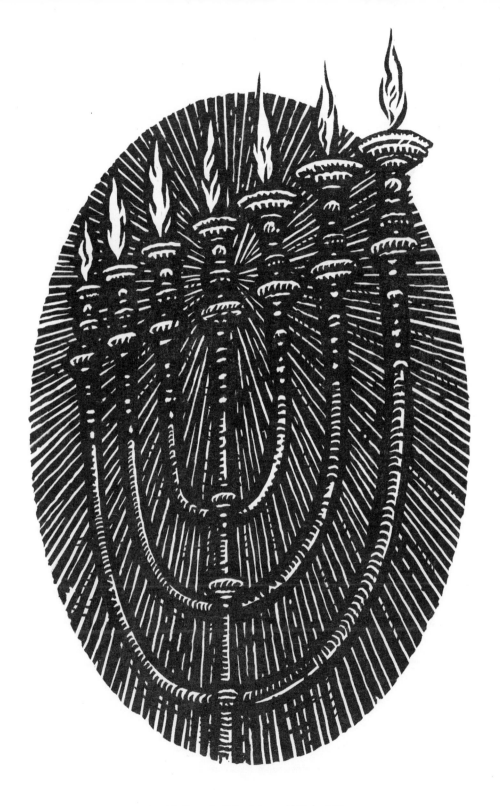

Day *16*: *"I am the light of the world." John 8:12*

YOUR VERY EARLIEST NIGHTMARES as a child left you clamoring and crying through the pitch-dark and the terror, longing for someone to just turn on the light.

Light is no light or trite comfort.

Light is one of our first and deepest comforts.

Without light, there is no hope of life within. If the sun burned out this instant, it would take eight-and-a-half long minutes for our world to go pitch-dark as the last bit of priceless sunlight traveled across the expanse of the universe to Earth. Within a week of darkness, the average surface temperature of Earth would drop below 0°, or −17°, and within a year, the average surface temperature of the ice-coated planet would plunge to well below −100°F.[1] You could skate across the ocean in the thick, inky dark, not one plant surviving anywhere on the frigid rock of Earth . . . and eventually not one human.

Nothing matters more to life on this planet than the light from the heavens. All life comes from light.

The only way to rightly read our reality, to understand where we are standing, is by light. Ask anyone trying to walk across a room in the middle of the night.

Light unveils truth.

After Jesus was interrupted by those who accused the woman caught in adultery, after lifting her chin, lifting her shame, lifting her sin-burden, He turned back and taught truth again to the people celebrating the Feast of Tabernacles, celebrating how God had provided for them when they wandered in the wilderness without crops or homes or much hope, celebrating how, in the middle of their dark wilderness, God had come as a pillar of fire. The people of God would never forget, never not celebrate how they had been between a rock and a hard place—between the overwhelm of the Egyptian army and the overwhelm of the Red Sea waves. God shattered their dark and entered in as a blazing tower of hope to shine the way through everything and lead them through.

And now, during the seven-day Feast of Tabernacles, held during harvest, God's people gathered at the Temple, night after night, for a ceremony known as the Illumination of the Temple, where it was "the custom during the first night, if not during every night, of the feast of tabernacles, to light up two large golden chandeliers in the court of the women, the light of which illuminated all Jerusalem".[2] And with the magnificent candelabras blazing, flickering light all across the cobbled streets of Jerusalem, the Temple orchestra would erupt in music and the people would swirl in worshiping dance through the torch-lit dark.

It was the last night of the Feast of Tabernacles. The candelabras were coming down. The dark was again growing large in the Temple. The cold absence of the glorious light of God was felt not just in the Temple courts but in the dark chambers of every human heart.

And then Jesus spoke these cosmos-shaking words in the Temple courts, and through all our dark, hopeless places: "I am the light of the world."

Standing there, after facing opposing accusers, after opposing darkness, after hundreds of years of Temple shadows, Glory Himself flooded the Temple and filled the whole world. And through the smothering dark of all our worst nightmares, the Light of the World turned on.

It happened exactly as the prophets foretold, and the inky pitch of humanity's existence was awakened in a wave of light: "The people walking in darkness have seen a great light; on those living in the land of deep darkness a light has dawned" (Isaiah 9:2).

The Word who came in the flesh to dwell among us is the Light of the World. The One who said, "It is I" and walked across the chaos of the night waves is the Light of the World. The I Am, the Bread of Life who fills us with the very vitality of being alive, is the Light of the World. How can we see the real spiritual reality? *Come and see Jesus.*

The Light of the World isn't some candlewick in a tunnel, some sequin-y star who steps into the limelight and tap-dances to dazzle; this is the very glory of God come to flood the earth. This glory enters the most shadowed recesses of our despair and pain with a light that ruptures all the dark with blazing hope and can never, ever be overcome by any news, any heartbreak, any hopelessness, any dark of this world.

It is only because Jesus is the Light of the World that we have ever recognized shadows, recognized evil, recognized suffering, recognized darkness. It's only when we see the actual goodness of light that we can identify what a shadow is, what evil is, what darkness is, what suffering is. Without ever experiencing the goodness of light, the darkness would just be the reality of our existence.

Christ is the only real Light of the World; He is the light that rightly illuminates lies, the truest light that unveils Truth, the sole guide to light the way. The One who is the literal Light of the World is the only Way, the only Truth, the only Life.

The Light of the World lights up how with Him there is no middle ground. All else is stumbling by the derivative light of the moon. Only when you turn to Jesus do you feel the warmth of the sun.

At the beginning of the Feast of Tabernacles, Jesus went up a mountainside and His face shone in the dark like the sun, radiant and brilliant. The disciples woke to witness a resplendent Jesus, lit like lightning, speaking to Moses and Elijah about what the original Greek reads as nothing less than Jesus' "exodus" (Luke 9:31).

Jesus is the exodus.

Jesus, who would go up to the Cross of Calvary, is the pillar of fire come down to be our only way out. Jesus, lit like the fire that flamed through the Red Sea waves, is the torch that makes possible the exodus out of our bondage and into the paradise of His presence.

Like there is no life apart from light, there is no love apart from light. It's only because Christ lights each day to the fullest that we can actually live the fullest life. Only when God is your light does your soul finally and fully grow. When you hide parts of your heart in the dark, you dance with the devil. But you get loved to life when you bring your whole self to the Light. When you live in the light of Christ, you can finally live fully awake—awake to His passion, awake to His love, awake to His justice, awake to His ways.

And now the Light of the World leans close to your heart as He whispers, *You're here to be a lit wick in the dark; you're here to be a lantern that's ignited by the only Light of the World* (Matthew 5:14). Any light we carry is derived from His divine light, and the only way to not be part of the darkness is to be lit on fire by Christ.

So the light of Jesus finds your eyes and assures you, "Whoever follows me will never walk in darkness, but will have the light of life." Let Christ live within and all other lights may go out, but when you live in Christ, there is a blazing ball of light within you that never dims.

As the preacher Spurgeon says, "If a man could travel so fast as always to follow the sun, of course he would always be in the light. If the day should ever come when the speed of the railway shall be equal to the speed of the world's motion, then a man may so live as to never lose the light. Now he that follows Christ shall never walk in darkness."[3]

When your gaze has been struck by the light of Christ, all there is to see is Jesus: You only see the imago Dei, the face of God, in everyone around you, and everyone around you sees the light of Christ in you.

There is real comfort here: When you live in the light of Christ, you never get to the end of the light. When you step into the darkness of the unknown, faith is knowing that the light of Christ is still guiding your every footstep.

This is the pilgrimage: Keep coming closer to the light of Christ, and don't resist. Let Him, the realest Light, keep coming closer to you, and don't turn away and be lured off into the dark by lesser loves and unsatisfying false lights.

You may fear the unknown in the dark, but there's one Light in the dark who knows you and the way through—so draw close to His warmth.

PERSONAL NOTES TO SOUL FROM TODAY'S PILGRIMAGE INTO THE HEART OF JESUS:

WHY YOU?

As he went along, he saw a man blind from birth. His disciples asked him, "Rabbi, who sinned, this man or his parents, that he was born blind?"

"Neither this man nor his parents sinned," said Jesus, "but this happened so that the works of God might be displayed in him. As long as it is day, we must do the works of him who sent me. Night is coming, when no one can work. While I am in the world, I am the light of the world."

After saying this, he spit on the ground, made some mud with the saliva, and put it on the man's eyes. "Go," he told him, "wash in the Pool of Siloam" (this word means "Sent"). So the man went and washed, and came home seeing.

His neighbors and those who had formerly seen him begging asked, "Isn't this the same man who used to sit and beg?" Some claimed that he was.

Others said, "No, he only looks like him."

But he himself insisted, "I am the man."

"How then were your eyes opened?" they asked.

Day *17: "So that the works of God might be displayed . . ." John 9:3*

He replied, "The man they call Jesus made some mud and put it on my eyes. He told me to go to Siloam and wash. So I went and washed, and then I could see."

"Where is this man?" they asked him.

"I don't know," he said.

JOHN 9:1-12

WHY YOU?

Why your family? Why your story? Why would a good God let that cancer rip through that body? Why would a good God snuff out that one fledgling dream? Why would a good God let that accident shatter your whole world, with no way to put any of the pieces back together again?

Why is life brutally overwhelming and then, blink, it's over?

Brokenhearted suffering is what happens to every single human heart in a broken world.

In the middle of all our questions and quests to find the answer to the questions of pain and suffering, what emerges are two frameworks: the blame framework and the shame framework.

The blame framework seeks to answer the problem of pain by asking all the questions: Was it his dysfunctional parents? Was it a malicious God? Was it the negligent, oppressive powers that be? Who is to blame for the ache of this pain?

Wherever pain goes, blame always stalks real close.

And for those of us who claim to follow Jesus, who take all our blame to the Cross, it can be tempting to drop our cross and shift all the blame back onto God. It can be easy to live like we've cut a deal with God, like we've signed up to live good in exchange for nothing bad to happen to us. So when life turns and cuts deep, we're ready to cut bait and bail, because God didn't keep His end of the deal. It's painfully tempting to scapegoat the Lamb of God.

The shame framework shifts the questioning from deciding who to pin the blame on to pinning all the shame within: Where did I go so wrong to deserve this? How did I sin? How did I fail? How bad am I for things to be going this bad?

Whatever begins with shame ends in soul-devastation.

Behind every question asking, "Why is there pain and suffering?"—underneath our blame or shame framework—is the heart cry, "Oh God, You owe me."

The problem of pain and suffering is ultimately a problem if you don't think a good God has actually made good on what He owes us. *Oh God, You gave me life and this moment and this breath and this heartbeat, and You owe me a better version of me—You owe me more ease, more carefree days. You owe me my life, done my better way.*

But what if there was a way for middle-of-the-night heart cries to change from "Oh God, You owe me" to "Oh Love, how You Love me"?

Is it possible that there's always, always, always some love of God to be found somewhere?

While it's very human to sit with the deepest ache of suffering and feel that no God sits with you in it, there's a way to waken to a gentle circle of comfort surrounding you, holding you close, and tenderly whispering love to your heart.

If your pain leads you to determine that there mustn't be any God, what you realize is this: Erasing God doesn't solve or erase any suffering. All it does is erase any and all hope.

To ask why there is suffering is to ask a moral question that assumes there is a natural law that defines something as evil. But if there is no God, then nothing is evil, nothing is actually suffering—everything is just survival of the fittest, and everything is just what it is. You can only ask the moral question about suffering and evil if you believe there is actually a moral being behind the universe to ask. Your heart only believes there should be justice if your heart actually believes that this universe was made to be just, that there is a Maker behind the universe who is just.

The disciples, with their blame and shame frameworks, looked at the man born blind and asked that very Maker of the universe, "Who sinned, this man or his parents, that he was born blind?"

The question of pain was flung in front of God in the flesh for Him: Was it blame? Or was it shame? Just tell us *why*.

"Neither," Jesus answered.

What if Jesus answered "neither" because that is the misdirected, simplistic question? What if the question isn't so much "Why this suffering?" but "Who is sovereign over this suffering?"

Tracing the heart of God is what begins to mend our heartbreak.

When we recollect who ultimately reigns over our suffering, the why of our suffering ultimately fades. Because our God is both sovereign Lord and safest Love, He is King, and He is loving-kind. God's presence isn't just loving; His very essence is Love. Love is who He is. Ultimately, what changes us from wanting a Q and A with God about our pain is to see how Love is God's DNA.

Ultimately, we only have one crisis. Our sole crisis is ultimately the crisis of our souls. Will our souls be abandoned forever, or will our souls be safe and loved forever? When we know that we are truly soul-safe in His great love for always, we realize that our greatest crisis is already truly over. Because of the Cross of Christ, our sole crisis, our soul-crisis, is over.

When you answer every one of your whys with *who*, you see what ultimately matters and how everything will be righted in the end.

"Neither," Jesus said. "This happened so that . . ."

Before He even finished the sentence, He said two words that explained the reason for or meaning in this suffering; He said two words that need to follow every iota of suffering.

So that.

This suffering happened . . . *so that.*

Suffering is never meaningless, pointless, purposeless. Suffering is *so that*. All suffering has the meaning of a *so that*.

God did not make the world so that there is pain, but when a broken world breaks our hearts, God works through that pain so that there is purpose even in all the tender mystery, so that there is always poetry in His intimate presence, so that His passionate love will love us to a deeper kind of a life of meaning, in the midst of the ache.

"This happened so that the works of God might be displayed."

The problem of pain isn't best answered with blame or shame but by entering into the mystery of it all—the mystery that makes it all about the glory of God on display.

What if suffering isn't so much a question to be solved but a quest for us to show love? "It is ours, not to speculate, but to perform acts of mercy and love, according to the tenor of the gospel. Let us then be less inquisitive and more practical," writes the theologian Spurgeon.[1]

What if we were less about endless attempts to break open some doctrinal kernels to find the answers to suffering and were more about the mystery of living broken and given, so more might taste the Bread of Life and the deep comfort of real love. Because isn't that what all the bravehearted and suffering are actually most starved for?

In the midst of every moment of our suffering, Jesus comes and says, "I Am"—*I Am here, right here.* Our suffering breaks the heart of Jesus—so deeply that He came to earth to enter right into our cracked hearts, to join us in the suffering, to take the suffering. Because of all the suffering in your story, Jesus stepped into history to take all your suffering on the cross, to begin revolutionizing and returning the order of the cosmos, ushering in the Kingdom of God that, even now, has begun undoing all the sadness and making our suffering only part of the story, not the end of the story. He sees your suffering, and He doesn't sit still; it's your crisis that drives Him to the Cross. His love always rushes to hold your lament.

Here in the pilgrimage is where your eyes can turn toward His love stretching out wide to you on the Cross, and all of us who were once blind can now truly see. The love in His eyes finds ours, and He speaks to the depths of our souls, loving us into a fuller kind of life: "Though he was God's Son, he learned trusting-obedience by what he suffered, just as we do" (Hebrews 5:8, MSG).

The human heart was made to meet His, not with a why but with hands, arms, and heart open wide and the trusting, steady beat: "Not as I will, but as you will" (Matthew 26:39).

This pilgrimage into real life always leans into the cadence of trust.

PERSONAL NOTES TO SOUL FROM TODAY'S PILGRIMAGE INTO THE HEART OF JESUS:

_____

_____

_____

_____

_____

_____

_____

_____

_____

_____

_____

_____

_____

_____

_____

_____

_____

_____

_____

_____

_____

_____

_____

_____

HE SEES
YOUR SUFFERING,
AND HE DOESN'T
SIT STILL;
IT'S YOUR CRISIS
THAT DRIVES HIM
TO THE CROSS.
HIS LOVE ALWAYS
RUSHES TO HOLD
YOUR LAMENT.

KNOWN

"Truly, truly, I say to you, he who does not enter the sheepfold by the door but climbs in by another way, that man is a thief and a robber. But he who enters by the door is the shepherd of the sheep. To him the gatekeeper opens. The sheep hear his voice, and he calls his own sheep by name and leads them out. When he has brought out all his own, he goes before them, and the sheep follow him, for they know his voice. A stranger they will not follow, but they will flee from him, for they do not know the voice of strangers." This figure of speech Jesus used with them, but they did not understand what he was saying to them.

So Jesus again said to them, "Truly, truly, I say to you, I am the door of the sheep. All who came before me are thieves and robbers, but the sheep did not listen to them. I am the door. If anyone enters by me, he will be saved and will go in and out and find pasture. The thief comes only to steal and kill and destroy. I came that they may have life and have it abundantly. I am the good shepherd. The good shepherd lays down his life for the sheep. He who is a hired hand and not a shepherd, who does not own the sheep, sees the wolf coming and leaves the sheep and flees, and the wolf snatches them and scatters them. He flees because he is a hired hand and cares nothing for the sheep. I am the good shepherd. I know my own and my own know me, just as the Father knows me

Day 18: "I am the door of the sheep." John 10:7

and I know the Father; and I lay down my life for the sheep. And I have other sheep that are not of this fold. I must bring them also, and they will listen to my voice. So there will be one flock, one shepherd. For this reason the Father loves me, because I lay down my life that I may take it up again. No one takes it from me, but I lay it down of my own accord. I have authority to lay it down, and I have authority to take it up again. This charge I have received from my Father."

JOHN 10:1-18, ESV

YOU ARE DEEPLY KNOWN . . . *and not alone.*

The way your thoughts wind through the neural matter of your mind, the way your hopes pulse through the chambers of your heart, the way you decide, the way you're tempted, the way you crave, the way you dream, the way you lean, the way you stumble forward—you are known. Like the triune God knew the Samaritan woman at the well, the way He knew who she had been with and when and how it had gone, Jesus wholly knows the whole of you. Jesus intimately knows His sheep—not merely as one in a collective flock, not as a string of faceless digits, not as a symbolic brand on some backside, but psychologically, emotionally, intellectually, spiritually, by actual, singular name.

The Maker of the Milky Way knows your name, calls you by name. Your name is on His lips.

How does a heart not burst into a supernova of joy?

When Jesus speaks the seven great "I am" statements in the book of John, the first few are not particularly relational, yet they are deeply provisional: "I am the bread," "I am the Light," "I am the door." But when Jesus turns and reveals His heart with the words "I am the Good Shepherd," the great I Am—the Word—reveals more of how He relationally feels about you.

He knows how you feel like you're the only one who gets it wrong quite like this and how you keep trying to mask the ways you fail. He's the omniscient One who sees every moment of the future, sees your every failure that will someday be, sees every falling and every heart fracture that's coming, and He only keeps coming to love you straight through to the very depths and back to a richer kind of life. Only when you honestly accept how you're much worse than you hoped can you look to the Cross and accept how much you're honestly worth to Him—and what He's honestly worth to you.

Whatever you've done won't ever lead to the undoing of God's love for you. Jesus keeps finding your eyes, holding up His scarred hands so you will believe Him: "I know my own and my own know me." No matter the painful story of your life, Jesus passionately gives His life for you, to re-story and restore the story of your life. Jesus is your one true Love, who knows everything that goes on in your heart and yet isn't going anywhere. The Shepherd who knows the whole of you does nothing less than wholly give Himself for you, and your worth is forever nailed down at the Cross. The God who spun out whole galaxies with the timbre of His voice— He cherishes intimate communion with you above all else. "In the Latin tongue the word for money is akin to the word 'sheep,' because, to many of the first Romans, wool was their wealth, and their fortunes lay in their flocks. The Lord Jesus is our Shepherd: we are his wealth," writes the sage theologian Charles Spurgeon.[1]

What greatly changes your heart is to see that your heart is the Shepherd's greatest treasure.

You are of such incalculable worth to Jesus that He gives His incalculably worthy life for you. When wolves come to steal, kill, or destroy His sheep, Jesus actually becomes a Lamb and offers Himself. "He was led like a lamb to the slaughter, and as a sheep before its shearers is silent, so he did not open his mouth" (Isaiah 53:7). Wolves may circle you, but Jesus becomes the Lamb instead of you, to protect you. A pack of hopelessness may stalk, but Jesus lays down as a Lamb for you, to preserve you. Jesus dies and gives His heart for yours so your heart can beat on forever.

Even in the midst of all that's brutally wrong within, what is in your heart is so unspeakably beautiful to Jesus that He willingly died an unspeakably brutal death to save it. God's holiness compelled Him to the Cross, and

God's justice drove Him to take the nails, but it was God's passion for you that kept Him there, so He could keep company with you for all eternity.

Jesus does more than save you from hopelessness; Jesus saves you for Himself. And in any given moment, Jesus is still giving Himself for you. Not for one moment, even now, has Jesus ever stopped giving His life for you. "He is able to save to the uttermost those who draw near to God through him, since he always lives to make intercession for them" (Hebrews 7:25, ESV). Jesus lives on to warrior on for you, to intercede for you, to advocate for you, to pray for you. Because God faced the worst death for you, you never face a hopeless day, a hopeless decision, or a hopeless death. He endlessly lives to give Himself endlessly for you, and you are rescued to the uttermost. If Jesus still lives for you, what could ever stop you from living for Him?

This is a world full of noise and voices and all kinds of amplified speakers, but you know you're His, because "the sheep hear his voice, and he calls his own sheep by name and leads them out." Even now, it's His voice that stirs your soul, His shepherding that keeps leading you out, His Word that keeps wooing you to the fullest life, and only His life that gives you life.

You do not need an abundance of days or an abundance of health or wealth or an abundance of power, prosperity, or perfection to have an abundant life. The abundant life is not about how much you have or how much you know but about who you know and how intimately you know Him. Which is to say: the only key to unlocking the abundant life is to intimately know God.

The abundant life is not having everything you want in life but abundantly enjoying the life you have in God and wanting to be with Him most.

To know God—and be known by God—is to live the most fulfilling life ever known. The timbre of His voice steadies the tentativeness of your soul, and the softness of your name on His lips calls you out of every shadow you've ever known.

When you hear His voice, it follows that you would want nothing more than to follow Him.

This is all there is to the abundant life, and this is everything. Whenever the enemy of the soul hisses that you're way behind, you get to exhale and say, "Of course, I'm behind, because Jesus is leading me—which means I'm fully on the way and right on time, because my heart is keeping time with His."

Because He leads you personally, He seeks nothing less than a personal relationship with you. This is profound wonder, a gentle truth: "For as many as are led by the Spirit of God, they are the sons of God" (Romans 8:14, KJV). He doesn't love you for a transactional business relationship; He doesn't love you for a polite acquaintance relationship; He doesn't love you for a shallow, lukewarm, apathetic relationship. He loves you to death and back to the most abundant kind of life for a relationship of intimate communion with Himself, the One who abundantly fulfills your every need. *He is love, and Love Himself means to live within you, to be your very life within.*

The Lamb of God protects you as His own and becomes your sacrificial lamb for every wolf in the shadows stalking you. Then He rises as the Good Shepherd to provide you with everything you need for abundant life in Him and to carry you safely all the way home.

The Good Shepherd believes you are worth it.

Every step of the pilgrimage, you can hear His voice asking: *Am I worth it for you?*

PERSONAL NOTES TO SOUL FROM TODAY'S PILGRIMAGE INTO THE HEART OF JESUS:

ONE

"I and the Father are one."

The Jews picked up stones again to stone him. Jesus answered them, "I have shown you many good works from the Father; for which of them are you going to stone me?" The Jews answered him, "It is not for a good work that we are going to stone you but for blasphemy, because you, being a man, make yourself God." Jesus answered them, "Is it not written in your Law, 'I said, you are gods'? If he called them gods to whom the word of God came—and Scripture cannot be broken— do you say of him whom the Father consecrated and sent into the world, 'You are blaspheming,' because I said, 'I am the Son of God'? If I am not doing the works of my Father, then do not believe me; but if I do them, even though you do not believe me, believe the works, that you may know and understand that the Father is in me and I am in the Father." Again they sought to arrest him, but he escaped from their hands.

He went away again across the Jordan to the place where John had been baptizing at first, and there he remained. And many came to him. And they said, "John did no sign, but everything that John said about this man was true." And many believed in him there.

JOHN 10:30-42, esv

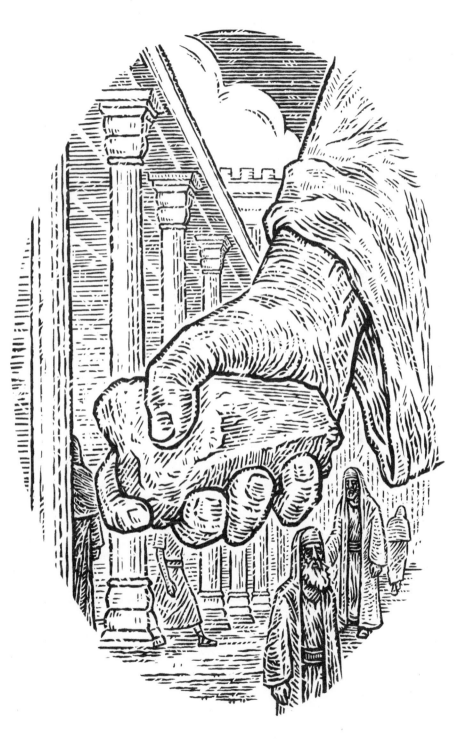

Day 19: "I and the Father are one." John 10:30

YOU KNOW THE ACHE of someone breaking their word to you.

You know the tender ache of someone breaking their promise and all the trust that shattered in a rain of pain.

And you can testify to it, too: Even hearts broken into a thousand aching shards can still keep beating and loving on.

Those highfalutin, self-assured leader-folks of Jesus' time had had enough. Jesus, the guy from Nazareth, had been proclaiming, "I am the bread, I am the Light of the World, I am the Good Shepherd, I am the door" as if He was God Himself, the great I Am—as if the cosmic King far beyond our touch had actually become one of us, to reach out and touch us. Who did this Jesus think He was?

Now He dared to say, "I and the Father are one."

In the Greek, it reads "one," not in the masculine, which would have meant "one person," but rather neuter in gender, which means Jesus and God are one in "essence."[1] One in unity, in purpose, in heart, in nature, in intention, in power. Jesus and God are one, and Jesus is God in the flesh. Essentially, the God of exploding stars slid on skin; the infinite became human. The Word who breathed out galaxies spoke on planet Earth and claimed deity, divinity, and utter supremacy.

The leaders of the day were irate. Yet Jesus' deity is not new news: "In the beginning was the Word, and the Word was with God, and the Word was God. . . . And the Word became flesh and dwelt among us" (John 1:1, 14, ESV). The Trinity may be a mystery, but Jesus has always been clear that He is God, the great I Am: "Jesus said to them, 'Truly, truly, I say to you, before Abraham was, I am'" (John 8:58, ESV).

This is not the first occasion that the leaders flew into a blind fury over Jesus' proclamations of who He is: "This was why the Jews were seeking all the more to kill him, because not only was he breaking the Sabbath, but he was even calling God his own Father, making himself equal with God" (John 5:18, ESV).

Jesus, while fully embracing His humanity, was fully asserting His deity, His authority, and His complete sovereignty. He stands alone in all of history:

- *Unique in entity:* None but Jesus has ever been both God and human (John 10:30).
- *Unique in prophecy:* No life but Jesus' was prophesied so clearly and accurately (Micah 5:2).
- *Unique in responsibility:* None but Jesus has ever come to save all humanity (Matthew 1:21).
- *Unique in Nativity:* None but Jesus was ever born of a woman of pure virginity (Matthew 1:23).
- *Unique in ability:* None but Jesus has the power to forgive immorality and iniquity (Mark 2:10).
- *Unique in reality:* None but Jesus has ever existed before time's chronology (John 1:1-2).
- *Unique in equality:* None but Jesus has experienced equality with God (Philippians 2:5-6).
- *Unique in sovereignty:* None but Jesus reigns sovereign for all eternity (Hebrews 1:8).

Because Jesus is unique in all of history, passionate worship of Him should not be unique; daily sacrificing for Him should not be unique; wholehearted surrender to Him should not be unique.

Yet why, ultimately, does it matter that the Father and Jesus are one?

Because the One who went to the Cross for you is no less than the very God who made you. Because Jesus and the Father are one, God doesn't just give His Son on the Cross for you; God gives God Himself on that Cross to be one with you. The only One who has ever loved us to death and back to the realest life actually wrote Himself into the ache of our story so He could live the fullest life we were supposed to live and rescue us from the death that was supposed to be fully ours. Because Jesus and the Father are one, the best way to understand what happens at the Cross is the "self-satisfaction of God through the self-substitution of God."[2]

The preeminent theologian John Stott says that Christ, "our substitute, then, who took our place and died our death on the cross, was neither Christ alone (since that would make him a third party thrust in between

God and us), nor God alone (since that would undermine the historical incarnation), but God in Christ, who was truly and fully both God and man and who on that account was uniquely qualified to represent both God and man and to mediate between them."

It ultimately matters that Jesus and the Father are one: "It is essential to affirm that the love, the holiness and the will of the Father are identical with the love, the holiness and the will of the Son. God was in Christ reconciling the world to himself."[3]

You aren't alone. Jesus understands that this mystery that He is both God and man is hard to believe, so He cups your face, pulls you close, and He tenderly pleads with your heart to consider all the works of His hand you've witnessed: "If I am not doing the works of my Father, then do not believe me; but if I do them, even though you do not believe *me*, believe the *works*, that you may know and understand that the Father is in me and I am in the Father."

He holds your gaze till you hear what He is telling you. If what He says about who He is eludes and bewilders you, then at least let all He *does* woo you to see that He is in the Father and the Father is in Him—and that God Himself is for you.

The leaders of the day understood what He was saying. They picked up what Jesus was laying down—the divinity He was claiming through His words—so they picked up rocks, coming up behind Him to silence Him. They reached for stones to crush bones, because they were of the thinking that it was better to break His blasphemy before it broke everyone.

About to be destroyed, pummeled to death by rocks mined from this rock of a planet that He'd made by the breath of His word, about to be executed by stoning, Jesus knew where to turn. When the moment turned to crisis, Jesus turned to the Word, answering them, "Is it not written in your Law . . . ?" There's no way to know when an everyday moment will turn to crisis and you'll need to know words by heart for your broken heart; you'll need to know what Scriptures to turn to. Why break open the Word when your heart is broken? Because in all the cosmos, in all this broken world, "Scripture cannot be broken." In a heartbreaking world, the only thing that cannot break is the Word.

Scripture cannot be broken, because *God cannot break His Word.*

The only Word in all the world that is unbreakable is the same Word that can't be unsubscribed to just because its truths are unpopular. The living Word is meant to be lived, to be experienced, so we can know how life-giving those words truly are. "In order to read the Scriptures adequately and accurately, it is necessary at the same time to live them," writes the theologian Eugene Peterson.[4]

As we live, the living Word, the One who "in the beginning was the Word" and who "became flesh and dwelt among us" gives us life, enlivens us, revives us, lives in us. And when the One who is the Word that cannot be broken lives within us, it begins to make us actually unbreakable.

Because the Word cannot be broken, the commands of the Bible can't leave us broken and crushed—they remake us more beautifully and fully alive, so that in the Word Himself, we are unbreakable. You know it; you can feel it. Because the Word is the only thing that cannot be broken, the Word is the only thing that can make us whole. The thing that cannot be broken is the very thing that can heal our brokenness.

Why do we not turn more often to the life-giving reviving of the only Spirit-Book in the world?

Because in a broken world, we get drawn to the adrenaline rush of the sharp edge of shards; we get addicted to the dazzling hits of novelty, the breaking news and noise of the headlines, the drama of the crash and the crush and the highlight reels. We say we want wholeness and peace, but in a broken world, we've normalized brokenness, because brokenness, in all kinds of ways, is part of what it is to be human. But to be fully, wholly human is to actually have union and communion with our Father, our brokenness finding wholeness in the unity of the Trinity.

And this healing journey toward our affirmation, transformation, soul-consolation, and God-adoration begins by daily turning the pages of the Word of God.

"The Holy Scriptures are our letters from home," writes Augustine.

What other words in all the world could mean more to our homesick broken hearts than actual letters from home?

To follow Jesus is to follow the Word—the whole of the Word, the authority of the Word, the supremacy of the Word, the unchangeability of the Word, the entirety of the Word. The Word may be disagreed with, but it can't be discarded, because there is no way to destroy the holy inspiration, indestructibility, and infallibility of it. Because God's character, God's heart, and God's goodness are constant—His Word is never contradictory.

God keeps His Word, and He gives us Himself so we can keep His Word.

The pilgrimage to life requires a map in hand, and God comes to that page with His very presence, and all our brokenness meets healing wholeness in the only One who is one with God, the only One who is the unchanging, unbreakable Word.

Every sacred page of the Word is heavy with the scent of this otherworldly love—the way of this pilgrimage to life.

PERSONAL NOTES TO SOUL FROM TODAY'S PILGRIMAGE INTO THE HEART OF JESUS:

GOD KEEPS

HIS WORD,

AND HE

GIVES US

HIMSELF

SO WE

CAN KEEP

HIS WORD.

IF HE HAD
BEEN HERE . . .

Now a certain man was ill, Lazarus of Bethany, the village of Mary and her sister Martha. It was Mary who anointed the Lord with ointment and wiped his feet with her hair, whose brother Lazarus was ill. So the sisters sent to him, saying, "Lord, he whom you love is ill." But when Jesus heard it he said, "This illness does not lead to death. It is for the glory of God, so that the Son of God may be glorified through it."

Now Jesus loved Martha and her sister and Lazarus. So, when he heard that Lazarus was ill, he stayed two days longer in the place where he was. . . .

Now when Jesus came, he found that Lazarus had already been in the tomb four days. Bethany was near Jerusalem, about two miles off, and many of the Jews had come to Martha and Mary to console them concerning their brother. So when Martha heard that Jesus was coming, she went and met him, but Mary remained seated in the house. Martha said to Jesus, "Lord, if you had been here, my brother would not have died. But even now I know that whatever you ask from God, God will give you." Jesus said to her, "Your brother will rise again." Martha said to him, "I know that he will rise again in the resurrection on the last day." Jesus said to her, "I am the resurrection and the life. Whoever believes in me, though he die, yet shall he live, and everyone who lives and believes in me

Day *20: Jesus said to her, "I am the resurrection and the life." John 11:25*

shall never die. Do you believe this?" She said to him, "Yes, Lord; I believe that you are the Christ, the Son of God, who is coming into the world."

When she had said this, she went and called her sister Mary, saying in private, "The Teacher is here and is calling for you." And when she heard it, she rose quickly and went to him. Now Jesus had not yet come into the village, but was still in the place where Martha had met him. When the Jews who were with her in the house, consoling her, saw Mary rise quickly and go out, they followed her, supposing that she was going to the tomb to weep there. Now when Mary came to where Jesus was and saw him, she fell at his feet, saying to him, "Lord, if you had been here, my brother would not have died." When Jesus saw her weeping, and the Jews who had come with her also weeping, he was deeply moved in his spirit and greatly troubled. And he said, "Where have you laid him?" They said to him, "Lord, come and see." Jesus wept. So the Jews said, "See how he loved him!" But some of them said, "Could not he who opened the eyes of the blind man also have kept this man from dying?"

Then Jesus, deeply moved again, came to the tomb. It was a cave, and a stone lay against it. Jesus said, "Take away the stone." Martha, the sister of the dead man, said to him, "Lord, by this time there will be an odor, for he has been dead four days." Jesus said to her, "Did I not tell you that if you believed you would see the glory of God?" So they took away the stone. And Jesus lifted up his eyes and said, "Father, I thank you that you have heard me. I knew that you always hear me, but I said this on account of the people standing around, that they may believe that you sent me." When he had said these things, he cried out with a loud voice, "Lazarus, come out." The man who had died came out, his hands and feet bound with linen strips, and his face wrapped with a cloth. Jesus said to them, "Unbind him, and let him go."

JOHN 11:1-6, 17-44, ESV

YOU NEVER CRY ALONE. Jesus weeps with you for every loss in your life, and Jesus rages with you against the night.

LOVED TO LIFE

And when Jesus heard that Lazarus was sick, He was anything but apathetic.

Lazarus and his sisters, Mary and Martha, knew how Jesus felt about them.

Jesus loved them.

They weren't bearing this suffering because Jesus couldn't bear them; they weren't desperate and despairing because Jesus was indifferent. Their loss was never because Jesus didn't love them. Loss never means that the Lord doesn't love you.

By the time Jesus made the less than two-mile trip from Jerusalem to Bethany, Lazarus was dead—for four stinking, excruciatingly long days. According to Jewish tradition in Jesus' time, a soul stayed near a body for three days and then departed. Did Jesus wait for four days so there would be no question that He alone was the source of Lazarus' miraculous resuscitation?

For all that is as rotting and far gone in your life as Lazarus, do you still wait on the ways of Jesus? For all the times when it seems like all hope has up and absconded and departed, do you still wait on a miraculous movement of God?

When Jesus finally arrived, Martha flung herself out the door and cried the ache of all humanity: "Lord, if you had been here . . ."

And Jesus' eyes found hers, steadied her, anchored her. She saw into the depths of the universe when He said words that reverberated in the ache of her heart and out across the whole of the cosmos: "I am the resurrection and the life. Whoever believes in me, though he die, yet shall he live, and everyone who lives and believes in me shall never die."

Those are the words that quake the darkest chambers of every heart awake. Those words explode awe over the deity, majesty, and centrality of Christ. The Word came to *be* those words: *I am the Life. Believe in Me, and you will live—fully live and never die.*

Only one kernel of trust that Jesus is the cosmic, great I Am who lays down His life to kiss the universe back to life is all the belief that is needed to rescue us and revive us back to life.

Only one mustard seed of trust that the eternal passion of Christ puts death to death, that His perfect love will slay the grave and raise you to the fullest life, is all the faith that is needed to resuscitate us into life without end.

Death shrivels in the face of this everlasting passion of God.

"Do you believe this?" Jesus asked Martha. And Jesus turns and asks you too.

Do you personally believe that Jesus can call life out of dead places of rotting dreams and decaying hope? Does your theology believe that, in the hands of God, dying things can become rising things? Do you believe that where you sit with wreckage, God starts resurrections? *Do you dare to believe this?*

Painful moments unveil our real theology. Painful moments give us the gift of seeing our personal need.

Ultimately, this is what matters most: Has your cerebral theology moved you to personal intimacy?

To really believe in something is to marry yourself to that idea. To strongly believe in something is to commit yourself to it, align yourself with it, wed yourself to it. To believe in Jesus as the resurrection and the life is to marry your life to Christ's.

Right theology of God always drives you to real intimacy with God.

When Mary was called to be with Jesus, she echoed the very same heart-howl as her sister, word for word, because this is the one cry all our theology has to wrestle with: "Lord, if you had been here . . ."

But Jesus didn't let the sonorous reverberation of His definitive power to slay death and bring life fill the caverns of Mary's aching heart. This time He brought life by murmuring a question of His own: "Where have you laid him?"

Where is he?

The question is a faint echo of the triune God's first ever recorded question in the Garden of Eden, His heart longing for the presence of Adam with the question "Where are you?"

Where could you possibly be if you're not here with Me?

God never stops asking where we are in relation to Him because He longs for a life-giving intimacy with us to steady us, fulfill us. The question we repeatedly ask of God is "Why? Why did you let this happen?" And the question God repeatedly asks us is "Where? Where are you in relation to Me, no matter what happens?" We only ask where God is because we long to ask Him "Why?" God asks where we are because God longs to be *with* us.

The real question isn't where God is in this, but where you are in proximity, intimacy, and vulnerability *with Him* through this.

In the midst of heartbreak and angst and ache, this is what changes everything: If God means everything to you, the witness of God changes everything for you.

When Someone who is your everything assures you they are unwaveringly with you through everything, nothing feels impossible and everything becomes surmountable.

However, if some random person you have little relationship with says they are with you, your emotions may not calm, your feelings may not regulate, you may not feel a deeper sense of safe at all. The truth is, someone's intimate closeness to you is what determines the worth of their witness. The greater your sense of intimacy with that person, the greater your sense of safety through whatever problem. If your covenant Person says they are with you, attending to your heart, your emotions are regulated, anchored, and safe. But if the witness of God doesn't profoundly *calm* your heart, then has God profoundly *captivated* your heart?

Your heart has wholly captivated His, for this is who He is: "When Jesus saw her weeping, and the Jews who had come with her also weeping, he was deeply moved in his spirit and greatly troubled. And he said, 'Where have you laid him?' They said to him, 'Lord, come and see.' Jesus wept."

Whatever our heartbreak, Jesus comes and Jesus sees and Jesus weeps.

Jesus didn't just enter into the world; Jesus intimately enters into *your* world, the world of your heart. Jesus, "a man of sorrows and acquainted with grief" (Isaiah 53:3, ESV), physically knows what it's like for a soul to groan, for a heart to howl. Your tears move Jesus to tears. No one in the history of the world has ever been more tender with the lines of your story than the Word Himself.

There is incomparable comfort in it: Jesus asks where you are, and He comes to be with you and weep with you, because the passion of

Jesus wants nothing more than to hold you through this. Jesus' sovereignty over everything may cover us, but it's Jesus' solidarity with us in everything that comforts us. The comfort we seek is found in the arms of the co-suffering God.

God weeps over what is altogether wrong before He ever begins to work all things together for good. Because God only knows: Shared tears always multiply healing.

But He does more than just weep; He feels more than just empathy with us in our grief. The God-Man is "deeply moved in spirit" not once but twice, both as He weeps with Mary and as He moves toward Lazarus' tomb. Mary's grieving tears leave Jesus "greatly troubled," the Greek verb for "greatly troubled" expressing a deeply felt passion, like a groaning within Himself. Some translators even render it as "a deep anger" that "welled up within him" (NLT).

What is this anger, this passionate feeling, this raw mixture of grief and groaning and fury that roiled within Him?

Jesus wasn't only weeping over Lazarus, because He knew He was about to miraculously raise a corpse that had been lying there putrefying for four days. Jesus wasn't just weeping for Martha and Mary, because He knew their devastated grief tears were about to turn to tears of delirious joy. What was happening was staggering: Jesus was seeing into the future, into every funeral that would ever be. And when Jesus stood by a grave on this planet, when Jesus' nostrils filled with the stinging stench of death, He saw you and He wept, furious over how losing your people would hurt you.

With tears blurring His whole world, Jesus stands with each of us who will ever stand at a funeral, weeping hard. He stands with each of us who are heartbroken, hating death as much as we do. Jesus is ferociously angry, to hell and back, with the horror and havoc of death for each of us.

In your every loss, Jesus weeps with you too. Through your every crucible, Jesus still comes to intimately love you. In your darkest valleys, feel how His furious love hates all kinds of death too.

Standing there with heart-shattered Mary and Martha, Jesus knew the surreal miracle that was about happen; He knew the funeral procession was about to be become a thrilling celebration; He knew how He's the resurrection and the life. But instead of telling Mary the breakthrough that was about to happen, Jesus, the weeping God, broke down with Mary. This is the very truest, realest love story that still happens: The wounds of our heart make the God of heaven weep. And our God will kill death to raise His own out of the depths. Yours is the powerful God, who is both the death-defying resurrection and the soul-fulfilling life. He is the passionate God, who weeps and rages and groans with us against death's dark night. It's His ministry of powerful hopefulness that revives us every day with resurrection hope, and it's His ministry of compassionate withness that comforts us with His consoling presence.

He knows you need one arm stretched out, pointing to the hope beyond, and He knows you need another arm wrapping 'round you, passionately holding on to you now. Jesus points to the truth of the resurrection and eternal life, and Jesus passionately weeps for all the griefs of life here and now. And we see how there is both a future hope and a present, intimate comfort right where you are.

Whatever suffering you're furious over, Jesus is furious too. However you're mad at the heartbreak in this broken world, Jesus is mad too. And because Jesus is mad at heartbreak, and because Jesus is madly in love with you, Jesus' passion for you drives Him to war against all the suffering in the world—*for you.*

To love is to suffer, which means that the only seeming way to end the problem of a world that suffers would be to have a world devoid of love and all the lovers. But your God, who is Love, puts on skin and enters the story of the world and the tender places of your story, and ultimately goes to the Cross to absorb all the dark and begin the revolution to end all suffering we have ever known. Jesus, who is Love and who loved the very most, suffered the very most to love you into the fullest life.

Dare to believe that belief in Him is the only way to really be alive.

Dare to keep honestly pilgrimaging toward Him.

Because Love Himself not only catches every single one of your tears; He also weeps with you, His tears watering a new way of being, a new way of life.

A resurrection.

PERSONAL NOTES TO SOUL FROM TODAY'S PILGRIMAGE INTO THE HEART OF JESUS:

NO ONE

HAS EVER BEEN

MORE TENDER

WITH THE LINES

OF YOUR STORY

THAN THE

WORD HIMSELF.

POURED OUT

Six days before the Passover, Jesus therefore came to Bethany, where Lazarus was, whom Jesus had raised from the dead. So they gave a dinner for him there. Martha served, and Lazarus was one of those reclining with him at table. Mary therefore took a pound of expensive ointment made from pure nard, and anointed the feet of Jesus and wiped his feet with her hair. The house was filled with the fragrance of the perfume. But Judas Iscariot, one of his disciples (he who was about to betray him), said, "Why was this ointment not sold for three hundred denarii and given to the poor?" He said this, not because he cared about the poor, but because he was a thief, and having charge of the moneybag he used to help himself to what was put into it. Jesus said, "Leave her alone, so that she may keep it for the day of my burial. For the poor you always have with you, but you do not always have me."

When the large crowd of the Jews learned that Jesus was there, they came, not only on account of him but also to see Lazarus, whom he had raised from the dead. So the chief priests made plans to put Lazarus to death as well, because on account of him many of the Jews were going away and believing in Jesus.

JOHN 12:1-11, ESV

Day *21: The house was filled with the fragrance of the perfume. John 12:3*

YOU AREN'T TOO MUCH; you are never too much.

Because all your muchness is to love much, and no one can ever love too much.

The party Mary and Martha and Lazarus were throwing only six days before the Passover was to make much of the God-Man, who had brought the dead man back to life. There was Lazarus, reclining while dining, feasting on his new lease on life, and Martha, the hostess, bringing the heaping plates filled with steaming goodness.

And Mary brought how very much she loved Jesus in her pint of pure nard, more expensive than a year's worth of work, and she broke the bottle open, and the room filled with the fragrance of flagrant love.

She didn't restrict, limit, or obstruct her offering; she didn't try to rightly proportion how much Jesus was worthy of receiving.

You lose all wrong sense of miserly proportion and give extravagantly, gaining the right sense of proportion, when Jesus is your portion. Moved by a passionate love, Mary simply lived into the posture of bowed surrender to her Love.

It's only in a bowed posture of surrender that you can pour out your one beautiful heart.

Though that dizzyingly expensive pint of nard was her one saving hedge against disaster, Mary humbly surrendered her hedge and let Jesus be her one true hedge of protection. What Mary did was sacrifice all her worldly security for the security of an otherworldly love. And she could give up all she was holding on to for a sense of safety, because she was soul-safe in Jesus.

Because Jesus paid the greatest expense for you, why withhold your most expensive treasure from Him?

Mary loosened her hair, it mattering absolutely nothing whether anyone thought of her as loose, because she knew her chains had been loosed, because the depths of her love for Jesus had completely let loose. A married woman letting her hair down in public warranted divorce, and Mary divorced the world to be passionately committed to Christ alone. She unbound her hair and let it fall because she had no shame about falling in love with God. She didn't let culture dictate what she could and couldn't do, and she didn't curtail her life to fit into other people's neat boxes. The only thing that ruled her life was her passion for Christ.

Strands of her hair, drenched in the nard, rubbed the scent of commitment into the heels of His feet. The room may rebuke, the arrogant scoff, the high and mighty balk at anyone bending scandalously low. But only care what Jesus thinks, and all that matters is that Jesus' wholehearted love meets nothing less than your wholehearted love.

When the love of God fully inhabits you, you're no longer inhibited from loving flagrantly.

Go ahead, rend the heart, break the locked jar of your thoughts, pour it all out in tears, in words, in pounding prayers, in scrawled words across the journaled page. Let down your hair and pull down your mask and be real with the one real and intimate God.

You're unbound to convention when your heart is wholly bound to His.

You only let down your hair when you're home; you only let down your hair when you feel safe to be your truest self. Jesus is your one true home. Jesus is the one Person you can let your hair down with and be your whole self with—and feel how your whole self is wholly safe.

And honestly: Your love for Jesus is only inappropriate if it is ultimately conditional.

Your love for Jesus is ultimately conditional if there has to be a return on investment, if following Him has to be somehow profitable for you. The cost of claiming Jesus as your own is the cost of all of yourself. Your vision of the future, your life-map, your reputation, your status, your desires, your cravings, your quick dopamine hits, your comforts, your distractions, your coping mechanisms, your false gods, your idolatry—they are all the cost of committing allegiance and fidelity to the Lamb of God and being held soul-safe by His nail-scarred hands forever.

Who is willing to give anything for the One who gave everything for your very soul?

Mary gave up all her rights because the passion of Jesus had actually made her soul right.

Every servant, every bondslave had clearly protected rights that, by law, ensured they would never have to get right down and slip off anyone's shoes.

No one could be forced to demean themselves and touch anyone else's feet. But Mary gave up all her rights and gave herself to Jesus. Why hold back anything from the One who laid His back down on the altar of the Cross and sacrificed His own beating heart to save yours? Who serves God only as long as they can keep back some of their heart to pour into other passions? Who gives to God only as long as it's not jarringly expensive? Who follows God only as long as the cost isn't terribly humbling? Who claims God only as long as it profits them, furthers them, benefits them?

You have two options every day: be a Mary, delighting to pay the cost, or be a Judas, always positioning to profit self. The choice is always: Are you sold out for Jesus . . . or just a sellout?

It's true: Judases sit with Jesus. Judases talk to Jesus. Judases even walk with Jesus. But no Judas ever treasured Jesus more than his treasures. No Judas ever passionately poured out praise for Jesus.

But Marys? Marys give up their greatest treasure so absolutely nothing can get in the way of treasuring Christ. Marys love scandalously, lavishly, extravagantly, because that is what it looks like to be loved to life.

If you lavishly love Jesus, you live daily, lavish worship of Jesus. Because it's one thing to give Christ what you have; it's another thing to give Him *who you are.*

Like Mary, you can feel it, how there is nothing like bending low at the feet of Jesus, looking up into His eyes and whispering: "I take my hands off controlling my life, because You stretched out Your hands for me on the Cross. There is nothing You cannot ask of me, because You did more for me than I would ever dream of asking."

Even now, you've pilgrimaged close enough to His heart that you can break open your own heart, unbind every iota of what's holding you back, and pour out every ounce of your passionate muchness there at His feet.

This will change the direction of your feet, of your very life.

PERSONAL NOTES TO SOUL FROM TODAY'S PILGRIMAGE INTO THE HEART OF JESUS:

PALMS OF PRAISE

The next day the large crowd that had come to the feast heard that Jesus was coming to Jerusalem. So they took branches of palm trees and went out to meet him, crying out, "Hosanna! Blessed is he who comes in the name of the Lord, even the King of Israel!" And Jesus found a young donkey and sat on it, just as it is written,

"Fear not, daughter of Zion; behold, your king is coming, sitting on a donkey's colt!"

His disciples did not understand these things at first, but when Jesus was glorified, then they remembered that these things had been written about him and had been done to him. The crowd that had been with him when he called Lazarus out of the tomb and raised him from the dead continued to bear witness. The reason why the crowd went to meet him was that they heard he had done this sign.

JOHN 12:12-18, ESV

Day *22:* *"Hosanna! Blessed is he who comes in the name of the Lord!" John 12:13*

YOU GET TO ENTER; you get to go all the way in.

You don't get stopped; you don't get turned away.

Your name is written on the list. You get free and easy and always access to enter right into the inner sanctum, right into the chambers of the heart of the King of everything.

What would stop you from going in as often as you need?

What if so much of life feels hard because it's hard to trust that your very name is written in heaven, etched into the palm of His hands, scrawled right there across the walls of His heart? What can't be handled when your name is engraved on the hands of the King of the cosmos?

When you don't believe your name is written on Christ's hands, giving you direct access to His heart, you can end up carrying needless weight on your back.

It's that very King of everything who rode into the capital city of Israel, triumphant on a donkey. It's that very King of the universe the crowd was lauding on the streets of Jerusalem with their palm fronds, crying, "Hosanna! Blessed is He who comes in the name of the Lord, even the King of Israel!"

If He's the only One across all of time and cosmic space and history who ever raised an actual dead and decaying corpse like Lazarus, how could He not be the King of the cosmos? If He conquered the hideousness of death, surely, thought his followers, He could conquer any and all bloated political powers that be.

They say this is the way it always went: "When a city welcomed a victor with open arms without an exercise of power, it was expected that the victor would enter on a donkey and not on a horse."[1] This is exactly how conquering Jesus rode into Jerusalem—on the humble back of one braying, swaying donkey. But there will be a coming day when all the heights of heaven will open and King Jesus will ride in on a galloping white horse (Revelation 19:11-16), the conquering King over all, who doesn't bend His knee. "Then the LORD will go out and fight against those nations as when he fights on a day of battle," prophesied Zechariah, and on that great day, "his feet shall stand on the Mount of Olives" (Zechariah 14:3-4, ESV), which was exactly how King Jesus rode into Jerusalem—from the Mount of Olives, to do battle with death and darkness and despair.

In that moment, all the streets of Jerusalem were a moving crush of crowd and noise and scents. Josephus, the Jewish historian, described one Passover when almost three million pilgrims teemed through the streets of Old Jerusalem.[2] And in this midst of literally millions of tired pilgrims, there was a constant stream of more than a quarter of a million crying lambs being herded through the streets—lambs to be slain for Passover and the broken hearts of all the people.[3]

By function of Jewish law, each family had to live with their lamb for three whole days, holding it close, feeding it tenderly, sleeping next to it, feeling its warm breath, before laying hands on it—before looking it in the eye and laying all of their own sins on it and slitting its throat at twilight.[4]

On the back of a donkey, under a cheering banner of waving palm fronds, King Jesus made His triumphant entry surrounded by crying lambs. He Himself was the willing Lamb of God making eye contact with all the crying people.

This conquering King Jesus, who rode into Jerusalem on a donkey, surrounded by lambs, is the One we will see at the very end of time: "One of the elders said to me, 'Weep no more; behold, the Lion of the tribe of Judah, the Root of David, has conquered, so that he can open the scroll and its seven seals.' And between the throne and the four living creatures and among the elders I saw a Lamb standing, as though it had been slain" (Revelation 5:5-6, ESV).

The Lamb-King entered the streets of Jerusalem to be slain for every sin that has ever slain a heart.

The Lamb-King is the same Lion of the tribe of Judah, yet He fulfilled the prophecy of Zechariah 9:9, which all the people had been waiting for: "Behold, your king is coming to you; righteous and having salvation is he, humble and mounted on a donkey, on a colt, the foal of a donkey" (ESV).

This is the moment: Wave your palm branches high, because your King comes meek and lowly, lower than your lowest sins. You can bless the God of heaven with your praise.

Wave your palm branches high: The Lamb-King enters on a lowly, humble donkey, because no matter how low things have gone for you, no matter the depths of your humiliation, you now get to enter into the presence of the most high King. Your praise can delight the heart of the very One who made all light.

Wave your palm branches high: The Lamb-King has the compassion to console us in our heartbreak, and He has the lionhearted courage to lay His bare, willing neck down on the altar, under the edge of the serrated knife, where your own stiff neck should have been. Your praise touches the heart of the One who gave you His life to love you to life.

Wave your palm branches high for His Highness, the Lamb-King. His greatness is entering into weakness so we could enter into His courts, in spite of our weakness, and find ourselves mended, saved, remade. Nothing is more life-giving than giving God praise.

How easy it can be to praise Him only when things turn out your way and then harden a bit when things don't go your way. That's always the temptation, if the King doesn't meet your expectations.

If the Lamb-King doesn't work things out the way we want, we want to grab a piece of wood and a hammer and crucify someone, nailing down our own bloody way. You always get to choose whether you wave a palm branch in honest praise or a hammer in angry protest.

Yet the subversive truth is right there, as the crowd waves their palm branches: What brings healing peace is hosanna praise. What to hold on to on the hardest days is simply this: Christ comes in ways as unexpected as riding a lowly donkey . . . and the way to not miss seeing Him is to keep looking for Him in the ways you'd least expect Him.

When unlikely, lowly donkey moments are met with honest hosannas, you get to see your King, Jesus, even here. And the best way to shield yourself against despair is to raise your palms in praise.

The way to enter into the fullest life is always possible: "Enter with the password: 'Thank you!' Make yourselves at home, talking praise. Thank him. Worship him. For GOD is sheer beauty, all-generous in love, loyal always and ever" (Psalm 100:4-5, MSG).

Whatever hurt you're desperately wanting a way out of, whatever way of hope you're desperate to enter into, Palm Sunday takes your hand, holds it up, and shows you the way. The only way to the fullest life is to keep your palms open wide.

In the midst of holding space for authentic lament in our heartbreaks, there can be holding space for authentic hosanna praise—to let praise open your hands, open your eyes, open your ears, open your heart to God— which opens the door to fully living. Whenever you lift your hands to praise God, it's your heart that finds itself uplifted too.

Don't believe things can entirely change? Look at Palm Sunday—to Good Friday—to Resurrection Sunday. The way of things can rise . . . and fall . . . and rise again. And the way through the fullest life, regardless of things being hard in life, is to always keep giving thanks, always keep the palms open and raised in praise. Because of the infinite glory and other-worldly love of King Jesus, things can change, you can change, circumstances can change, everything can change.

This is your daily pilgrimage: You can open your palms in trust, especially now, and enter in.

You're as deeply committed to Jesus as you are to your daily adoration of Jesus.

PERSONAL NOTES TO SOUL FROM TODAY'S PILGRIMAGE INTO THE HEART OF JESUS:

LETTING GO

Now among those who went up to worship at the feast were some Greeks. So these came to Philip, who was from Bethsaida in Galilee, and asked him, "Sir, we wish to see Jesus." Philip went and told Andrew; Andrew and Philip went and told Jesus.

And Jesus answered them, "The hour has come for the Son of Man to be glorified. Truly, truly, I say to you, unless a grain of wheat falls into the earth and dies, it remains alone; but if it dies, it bears much fruit. Whoever loves his life loses it, and whoever hates his life in this world will keep it for eternal life. If anyone serves me, he must follow me; and where I am, there will my servant be also. If anyone serves me, the Father will honor him.

"Now is my soul troubled. And what shall I say? 'Father, save me from this hour'? But for this purpose I have come to this hour. Father, glorify your name." Then a voice came from heaven: "I have glorified it, and I will glorify it again." The crowd that stood there and heard it said that it had thundered. Others said, "An angel has spoken to him." Jesus answered, "This voice has come for your sake, not mine."

JOHN 12:20-30, ESV

Day *23*: *"Whoever loves his life loses it." John 12:25*

Let go of your life, to live. Let go of your grip, to grow. Let go of all the cheaper passions that have you bound to lesser loves, and let the passion of Christ lead you out of bondage and into bonding with the only Love that won't ever let you go.

Yet it's true: Letting go may not feel like thriving; letting go can feel terrifying. Letting go can actually feel a lot like falling.

But you can hear the unexpected voice from heaven, reverberating in your soul: *Unless you fall.*

There will be all kinds of fallings, all kinds of failings. There will be falling further away from Him, there will be falling into all manner of messy sins, there will be falling hard and breaking fragile hearts, and there will be more failings than your heart can ever dare or bear to count. But in the midst of all the falling, you get to become the small of a seed.

"Unless a grain of wheat falls into the earth and dies . . ."

Every falling is redeemed when you let it make you into a seed.

What feels like everything falling apart may be you becoming a seed falling into the earth, to break apart and grow into more.

What feels like everything falling apart can be exactly when you fall in love with God.

Let go, and let God grow you to life.

It was a day or two after Jesus' triumphant entry into Jerusalem, and He was teaching at the Temple.

Greeks who had heard of His signs, His miracles, His healings, His ways had come all the long way to hear the wisdom of the King of everything. While wise men had come from the East to the crèche at the beginning of the incarnation of God, now wise men from the West were coming at the end, before the Cross of the King, when He would sacrifice Himself for the salvation of humanity.

"And Jesus answered them, 'The hour has come for the Son of Man to be glorified.'" Christ was already glorious; He would become even more glorious through sacrifice. No matter how glorious Christ may be to us, there is always more of His glory to be unveiled to all who are willing to surrender self.

As Jesus emptied Himself, He was filled with the greatest glory; as He was obedient to self-death, He was raised to give life.

"The hour has come. . . . For this purpose I have come to this hour." In the language of God, time is for sacrifice; time is for letting go and living given; time is for self-dying so there can be real living.

Jesus looked over at the insiders angling to kill Him for raising a dead body because it threatened their hold on power. And He looked over at the outsiders, who were jockeying to hear Him because they marveled that anyone could hold the power to actually raise dead bodies to life. The moral-ladder climbers and the power hungry were undone by the kinds of "nobodies" Jesus kept company with, while all the down-and-outers' hurting bodies were remade when they let go and let His healing love touch them. And Jesus nodded and knew: This was why He came. Love came to revolutionize all thinking, all paradigms, all the ways this old world turns—*and turn us all around*. The Lamb, who is the Lion, who is Love, who is the King of everything, came to live out this paradox: The way to rising is descending, the way to flourishing is fully letting go, the way to great yield is to yield greatly. Let every falling make you into a seed.

If you live like a seed, what could break you becomes your breakthrough.

The way you become a seed of infinite possibility is to let go and die to self with humility.

But if the seed fails to die to self, the power of new life fails to unfold within. The Holy Spirit, the catalyst of new life, only moves and stirs where there is first self-dying. Wherever there is death to the self-life, the divine life flourishes.

This is always the paradox of the Kingdom of God: Unless we are dying daily, there's no living fully. Escapism must die, numbing must die, self-sufficiency must die, addictions must die, lesser loves must die. Anyone who passionately loves their life more than they passionately love Jesus will lose it. Live for yourself, and you do not really live.

But lose your life to love, and you'll fully live; live for God and others, and you'll live an otherworldly, fulfilling life. "Seek first his kingdom and his righteousness, and all these things will be given to you as well" (Matthew 6:33). The way to gain more is to live given; the way to fully live is to die daily; the way to everything you seek in life is through living a cruciform love that's willing to surrender.

For Jesus, you were worth loving to death, worth falling into the earth and dying for, so He would not remain apart from you. Because Love would rather die first than let that happen. "Without his people Jesus would have been a shepherd without sheep. . . . He would have been a husband without his spouse; but he loves his bride so well that for this purpose did he leave his Father and become one flesh with her whom he had chosen. He clave to her, and died for her; and had he not done so he would have been a bridegroom without a bride. This could never be," wrote Spurgeon.[1]

This is everything: Christ's dying is the life of the world. All the realest life in the world is really the fruit of Christ's death.

If the reason Jesus came was for His mentoring or His moral example, His life alone wouldn't have produced great yield in the world; rather, Jesus, by His own testimony, declared that unless He died, His life would not bring forth genuine fruit. It was not Jesus' example or His expositions or His exhortations that saved us to life—it was only the expression of His love on the Cross that could love us to life. Because neither His example nor His exhortations can erase our sin and errors—only His sacrificed love can do that. His teaching is not ultimately the door into the fullest life; it is His death and atonement on the Cross that is the only door to *at-one-ment* with God, which is always the realest life.

How can the passion of Christ not move the heart to deeper passion? How can Jesus' humble, unlikely journey, riding on a donkey, heading to the sacrificial love of the Cross, and then to His Father, not prompt us to follow His footsteps of that dusty pilgrimage to wholeness and flourishing?

Gazing long on His arms stretched out in cruciform love, you can feel your heart stirred, stoked, drawn. And Jesus whispers, "And I, when I am lifted up from the earth, will draw all people to myself."

Jesus wasn't speaking of the lifting up of His resurrection or the lifting up of His ascension—Jesus was speaking of laying Himself down on the cross, of going down into the tomb, of being crushed like a seed in the earth—and then being lifted up, raised up. In the upside-down ways of

God, the humiliation of being laid down on the cross becomes being lifted up for the glorification of God.

It's striking: When you truly love the eternal things of God, it looks like you're openhanded with the fleeting, material things of this world.

And unless Jesus draws your attention, draws your attraction, draws your affection, draws your heart, where exactly have you drawn Jesus in the landscape of your life?

If your attention is drawn time and again, day after day, more toward lesser loves than to Love Himself, have you drawn for yourself a lesser life?

A full surrender of everything to Love Himself is the only way to pilgrimage into the fullest life.

PERSONAL NOTES TO SOUL FROM TODAY'S PILGRIMAGE INTO THE HEART OF JESUS:

PEOPLE OF THE TOWEL

It was just before the Passover Festival. Jesus knew that the hour had come for him to leave this world and go to the Father. Having loved his own who were in the world, he loved them to the end.

The evening meal was in progress, and the devil had already prompted Judas, the son of Simon Iscariot, to betray Jesus. Jesus knew that the Father had put all things under his power, and that he had come from God and was returning to God; so he got up from the meal, took off his outer clothing, and wrapped a towel around his waist. After that, he poured water into a basin and began to wash his disciples' feet, drying them with the towel that was wrapped around him.

He came to Simon Peter, who said to him, "Lord, are you going to wash my feet?"

Jesus replied, "You do not realize now what I am doing, but later you will understand."

"No," said Peter, "you shall never wash my feet."

Jesus answered, "Unless I wash you, you have no part with me."

"Then, Lord," Simon Peter replied, "not just my feet but my hands and my head as well!"

Jesus answered, "Those who have had a bath need only to wash their feet; their whole body is clean. And you are clean, though not every one

Day 24: *"You should do as I have done for you." John 13:15*

of you." For he knew who was going to betray him, and that was why he said not every one was clean.

When he had finished washing their feet, he put on his clothes and returned to his place. "Do you understand what I have done for you?" he asked them. "You call me 'Teacher' and 'Lord,' and rightly so, for that is what I am. Now that I, your Lord and Teacher, have washed your feet, you also should wash one another's feet. I have set you an example that you should do as I have done for you. Very truly I tell you, no servant is greater than his master, nor is a messenger greater than the one who sent him. Now that you know these things, you will be blessed if you do them."

JOHN 13:1-17

YOUR MANUAL FOR THE FULLEST and most exuberantly alive kind of life is unexpectedly simple: Life is about passion.

Life is about the passionate love that is willing to suffer, to sacrifice, to serve, to live given, to be, in all things, cruciform.

Love that goes low lifts everyone high.

Love that kneels down raises everyone up.

Love that bends is what straightens things out.

The God-life has only one trajectory: downward mobility.

It was just before the Passover. Jesus and His disciples leaned around a triclinium, U-shaped and low to the floor. Everyone was dirty and propped up on pillows, and dusty feet were all around.

It's far easier to *judge* someone's dirt than to help *wash away* someone's dirt.

It's more tempting to point out how someone has been in the muck and the mire than to bend down with a basin and wash away someone's stain.

The way of love is not to condemn someone for their story but rather to commit to the work of restoring and re-storying them.

This is the way of your servant-King: Jesus laid aside both His heavenly glory and His outer garment to robe Himself in humanity and wrap

Himself in a towel. The heart of the King of the universe is the heart of a sacrificial servant. "The form of God was not *exchanged for* the form of a servant; it was *revealed in* the form of a servant. In the washing of their feet the disciples, though they did not understand it at the time, saw a rare unfolding of the authority and glory of the incarnate Word, and a rare declaration of the character of the Father himself."[1]

This is who God is: God in human flesh took on the likeness of a servant—because a servant is who He is—to love the unlovely to life. God came down and God bent down, because the passion of God always goes lower to lift up the downtrodden. Right in this moment, right now in your life, you are being lifted, you are being raised, you are being washed clean, you are being renewed.

This is why Jesus bent low: to take the crushing weight of all history and humanity, everything you've saturated with tears, every heartbreak you've carried, and every manner of ache you've held. He came to take it all on His back. What's been over your head is borne in His heart. What's been a millstone around your neck is borne in the palms of His hands.

All brokenness, all sin has to go somewhere in the world. If someone doesn't pay the price for sin, sin never stops exacting the cost. Somebody has to bear the price of sin, or we will all keep bearing the scars. Either sin keeps breaking hearts, or it's absorbed into Christ's heart. Either it keeps bruising and busting and breaking lives and hopes and hearts, or it's absorbed in the passion of Christ on the Cross. Sin will not be stopped—it can only be absorbed and washed clean in the cruciform love of Jesus.

The cruciform love of Jesus bears the crush and cost of all your pain to be your way into expansive, bona fide freedom. He loved His own to the very last earthly heartbeat of His life, to the very uttermost.

For God-with-skin, all that's on His bucket list is to make the bucket into an act of sacrifice, of service, of suffering love. Instead of completing a bucket list in His last hours, He took a bucket of water and lowered Himself to wash the feet of His friends and complete this sacrificial act of love for them—for *you*. In nearly twenty-four hours, the Lamb-King would hang on the cross. Who spends their last hours making themselves last? In His last hours, Jesus lived as He died, putting others first.

He would be abandoned by His own, *yet He loved them*. He would be forsaken by His own, *yet He loved them*. He would be betrayed by His own, *yet He loved them. Yet He loves you.*

Jesus poured the water into a bowl, like He would pour out His lifeblood on the Cross. He washed the filth from the feet of the disciples, like He washes filth from your life, your mind, your soul.

In the basin's dirty water, Jesus can see your face, and you can see His. Gaze long on His face full of love for you. Jesus holds your feet—feet battered and bruised by the valleys and all that's been rocky and steep. Jesus holds your feet—feet that have carried painful weight, feet that have been tied up in that which didn't fit and was too tight.

You can risk how it feels to sit with being exposed and in need.

There is no shame. There is no shame now.

The grime that's left stains, that can't be scrubbed away, the embarrassment of how things have gone madly different from the way you wildly imagined—none of it makes Him pull back or take even one of His promises back. Jesus doesn't ever shrink back from your grime, and you never have to shrink back from His grace.

It's no small thing—it's everything to let Jesus wash your feet even now, to receive the touch of His towel, to receive impossible grace, to simply receive. This is an act of humility. Humility isn't only about giving love to others; humility is about being ready to receive love yourself. You get to be passionately loved. You get to be completely clean.

Look long at the love of Jesus for you right now. Linger here.

How could you live anything less than as a servant, because this is how you love and thank Him? How could you not become one of the people of the towel when you've been touched by His holy towel? How could you ever think of throwing in the towel when sacrificial, cruciform love seems hard—when Jesus invites us to be people of the towel so love can be seen?

Jesus bent down with a basin and embodied love for us, incarnated the blueprint to the fullest life. This act of washing feet, this act of service, this act of givenness "is a parable in action, setting out that great principle of lowly service which finds its supreme embodiment in the cross."[2]

That is what this is: This is a passion parable. This is a love story—about being loved to life. Jesus ultimately makes His life into the bucket that He pours out to the bottom for you to be washed into new life. And now you get to pour out your heart, too, so others can fully live.

Who needs to be washed with a tender, reviving grace?

Feel how your Love hands you a towel.

What if, on your deathbed, your hands were chapped and your heart was enlarged from a life of all kinds of foot washing, from a life of reaching out with all kinds of cruciform love? Wouldn't that be proof of a life truly lived?

What would it look like, even right now, to love someone passionately, sacrificially, so you might live—and die—fully fulfilled?

What could be a more meaningful pilgrimage?

PERSONAL NOTES TO SOUL FROM TODAY'S PILGRIMAGE INTO THE HEART OF JESUS:

LOVING
THE IMPOSSIBLE

After saying these things, Jesus was troubled in his spirit, and testified, "Truly, truly, I say to you, one of you will betray me." The disciples looked at one another, uncertain of whom he spoke. One of his disciples, whom Jesus loved, was reclining at table at Jesus' side, so Simon Peter motioned to him to ask Jesus of whom he was speaking. So that disciple, leaning back against Jesus, said to him, "Lord, who is it?" Jesus answered, "It is he to whom I will give this morsel of bread when I have dipped it." So when he had dipped the morsel, he gave it to Judas, the son of Simon Iscariot. Then after he had taken the morsel, Satan entered into him. Jesus said to him, "What you are going to do, do quickly." Now no one at the table knew why he said this to him. Some thought that, because Judas had the moneybag, Jesus was telling him, "Buy what we need for the feast," or that he should give something to the poor. So, after receiving the morsel of bread, he immediately went out. And it was night.

When he had gone out, Jesus said, "Now is the Son of Man glorified, and God is glorified in him. If God is glorified in him, God will also glorify him in himself, and glorify him at once. Little children, yet a little

Day 25: "Lord, who is it?" John 13:25

while I am with you. You will seek me, and just as I said to the Jews, so now I also say to you, 'Where I am going you cannot come.' A new commandment I give to you, that you love one another: just as I have loved you, you also are to love one another. By this all people will know that you are my disciples, if you have love for one another."

JOHN 13:21-35, ESV

YOU KNOW HOW you once cracked jokes with them; did life with them? How you made loud, laughing memories with them around tables, had real bonds of friendship with each other, and you actually thought you'd always be there for each other, have each other's backs, be in each other's corner always?

But it turns out . . . the joke's kinda on you, and they ended up seeing some situation entirely differently from the way you do or have some different political point of view. Or maybe they wanted things to go down differently, or they think you should somehow be someone different or do things another way.

It's okay to say you feel deeply betrayed.

It's okay to honestly confess: Betrayal doesn't just leave your heart broken; it leaves your soul jaded.

It's okay to quietly say it: It's harder to give forgiveness to a close friend than to someone who never was a friend. Because when trust was deep, the feeling of betrayal cuts deeper.

Your Jesus knows what it's like to have your own Judas.

Jesus wasn't betrayed by some Tom, Dick, or Harry down the street; Jesus was betrayed by one of His very closest friends—one who kissed Him warm on the cheek and then turncoated on Him, leaving Him out in the cold to be crucified alone.

It was on Thursday of Holy Week, Maundy Thursday, when Jesus sat at the Last Supper. On each side of Jesus sat one of His disciples. One of them was the one "whom Jesus loved"—the way John refers to himself four times in his Gospel. Once here, in the upper room, where Jesus bent Himself low and washed everyone's feet, once at the cross of Calvary, before the Passion of God (John 19:26), once at the empty tomb (John 20:2), and once with the resurrected King at the Sea of Galilee (John 21:20). Each time, he speaks of being the one whom Jesus loved—because John was hidden in the love of Jesus. There is no way to really fully live apart from being hidden in the passionate love of God.

While on the one side of Jesus sat "John the divine, [on] the other was Judas the devil. One of them was the seer of the Apocalypse, the other was the son of perdition," writes Spurgeon.[1] Jesus was flanked by John, who was leaning against the heartbeat of Jesus, and Judas, who was just against Him. But Jesus' love presses against those who are against Him: While we were yet sinners, while we hated Him, Jesus loved us to death, so we could really live (Romans 5:8), and He loves to death exactly those we struggle to live with. While we were yet struggling to live with the difficult, *Christ died for them.*

It changes your heart when you know Christ died for those who've hurt your heart.

The love of God doesn't become lesser but grows greater in the face of great heartbreak. As God-with-skin-on bent low with a basin of slopping water to wash dirty feet to show us the way of passionate love, He would now hand the dipped sop of bread to Judas.

Like Jesus sopped the bread and passed it to Judas, so we drown all evil in an ocean of grace.

If Jesus could dip from the same bowl as Judas and then pass along the bowl with grace, how can we who have been washed in the grace of Christ not find ways to pass on all the grace we've known? How can we not pass on the goodness of the grace we've tasted?

Jesus finds your eyes in this moment and whispers the mandate "A new commandment I give to you, that you love one another: just as I have loved you, you also are to love one another. By this all people will know that you are my disciples, if you have love for one another."

Turns out: You only get to be known as a disciple if you're known for your cruciform love.

It's possible, with love: You can take any closed door and make it into an open table.

It's possible, with cruciform love: Where there is a relational break, instead of breaking fellowship, you can break open the heart in prayer and ask the Lord if there is a safe way to somehow break bread together.

It's possible, with surrendered, cruciform love: You can live by just eight words: *Love one another just as Christ has loved you.*

This is what happened on Maundy Thursday of Holy Week: On the night Jesus was *betrayed*, Jesus found ways to still *be Love*.

Your life, too, has known all kinds of betrayals: the night when the prodigal sliced open your heart, the night when your boss betrayed your trust and you lost your job, the night when your person said words that can't be unsaid and stomped out the front door, the night when the toilet stopped flushing and the dog puked all over the back mat, the night when all your hopes and your everyday life seemed to betray you, the night when it looked like dawn would never come again. Even on those nights, the people of Jesus can still give thanks for the closeness of Jesus, the comfort of Jesus, the compassion of Jesus, the kindness of Jesus, the kinship of Jesus.

When Jesus had to fight through the dark, staring right into the most impossible situation of the Cross, abandoned by His circle of friends, what did Jesus do? Out of a universe of supernatural options at the tip of His fingers, what did Jesus determine was the most revolutionary way forward?

On the night when Jesus was betrayed, He gave thanks.

If Jesus can give thanks in that, might it be possible to give brave thanks in anything? If Jesus can give thanks in that kind of heartbreak, how can we not find ways to give thanks even in ours?

And when it's brutally, impossibly hard? Jesus comes and sits down beside you.

He breaks this bit of soft bread, and we can feel it—how our broken hearts soften too. He reached out with one hand to hand the bread to Judas, and with the other hand, He hands the bread to us.

We are all the Judases who have betrayed Jesus too.

And what can we do but take the bread and murmur our heartfelt thanks, too, and reach out and sacrificially love too?

This is no less true: Because of the night Jesus was betrayed, we can give thanks too. We give thanks that He gives grace to Judases like us. When we reflect on how great our own sins are, how can we not have great gratefulness and great grace for every other broken sinner? When we know how much grace we've been given to cover our own betrayals of Jesus, how can we not give others grace for theirs?

After Jesus was marked with scars and left this world, love would be the mark of His people, to leave a mark on the world.

Because of love, life can come.

And Jesus showed us that loving forgiveness is always the most life-giving.

As Judas walked out of the upper room, Jesus turned toward the Cross. He knew what lay ahead—arrest and trial and torture, humiliation and condemnation and crucifixion—and Jesus called this kind of sacrificial love nothing less than glory.

Heartbreak and hardship are not hindrances to our love for God but are often the catalysts that make us fall into the arms of His love.

While the world might look and say, "How terribly crucified," those living in the love of Jesus can trust that miraculous good can come out of even this, and say, "Still beautifully glorified."

The mandate of those who follow Christ is to live the passion of Christ—to love every day we're on earth, like Jesus loved us to death on His last day on earth. This is the way to rise to new life every day, to make the cadence of our days just this refrain: "As Jesus has loved me . . ."

As Jesus has loved me, let me take care of that for you. As Jesus has loved me, let me give you not just the benefit of the doubt but amazing grace. As Jesus has loved me, let me forgive you. As Jesus has loved me to life, let me love you with my life.

As we love each other as Christ loves us—even those who have broken our hearts—we end up loving others far more than we ever thought possible, because we feel how we are loved by Christ far more than we could ever imagine. The forgiving love of Jesus gives us a way to keep miraculously giving love, especially when it seems impossible.

Pause in the midst of your brave pilgrimage toward true life, and there it is: Give thanks for God's grace, even in your hard places, and you see you actually have more than enough of God's grace to pass on to others in theirs.

PERSONAL NOTES TO SOUL FROM TODAY'S PILGRIMAGE INTO THE HEART OF JESUS:

AFTER

JESUS WAS

MARKED WITH

SCARS,

LOVE WOULD BE

THE MARK OF

HIS PEOPLE.

THE WAY

"Let not your hearts be troubled. Believe in God; believe also in me. In my Father's house are many rooms. If it were not so, would I have told you that I go to prepare a place for you? And if I go and prepare a place for you, I will come again and will take you to myself, that where I am you may be also. And you know the way to where I am going." Thomas said to him, "Lord, we do not know where you are going. How can we know the way?" Jesus said to him, "I am the way, and the truth, and the life. No one comes to the Father except through me. If you had known me, you would have known my Father also. From now on you do know him and have seen him."

JOHN 14:1-7, ESV

Day 26: "I am the way." John 14:6

HOW IN THE WORLD do you find the best way through to the fullest, realest life—with your only life? Let not your heart be troubled. Let not your heart be agitated with any worry in this world, but let your heart be stirred with affection for Jesus, the love of your life.

The seemingly outlandish claim, out of the mouth of the King of everything—"I am the way, and the truth, and the life. No one comes to the Father except through me"—can only come from One who isn't from anywhere within the walls of this world, from the only One who can untrouble our hearts with an otherworldly peace.

Perhaps nothing Jesus said is more comforting—or more controversial.

Who could audaciously say that they alone are the truth, the way, the life?

As the story goes, aren't we all like someone who is blind, reading along the skin of an elephant like braille, certain that the whole elephant is just like the leg we are feeling along or the tail or trunk we've touched? Until the only seeing person, the King, truthfully tells us that the elephant is a large beast and we've each touched only one part. As Lesslie Newbigin challenges, "If the king were also blind there would be no story. The story is told by the king, and it is the immensely arrogant claim of one who sees the full truth which all the world's religions are only groping after. It embodies the claim to know the full reality which relativizes all the claims of the religions and philosophies."[1] Which is to also quietly offer: If anyone claims that no one can actually have the whole truth, are they themselves audaciously assuming they have the superior knowledge and the whole truth about the truth?

And, as Greg Koukl writes, "This is a factor the illustration doesn't allow for: What if the elephant speaks? The claim of Christianity is that man doesn't learn about God by groping. Instead, discovery is through God's own self-disclosure."[2]

God doesn't just leave us to bumble along, reaching for a part of Him. Our God speaks. The dialect of God is Jesus, and His tongue is truth.

Of all history's great sages, only One speaks truthfully from His lips, "I am the way."

Many have helped people live better lives, but there's only One who can take us on a pilgrimage from being the walking dead to living the actual realest life. In a world that claims all truth is merely relative, only One is the singular truth. Only a Man who is deity Himself could make such a decree. And in only a handful of years, this anchored belief in who Jesus really is would move countless people to their knees in adoration of Jesus as actual God on high, the Way, the Truth, the Life.

Because when a dead man had been four days rotting in a tomb, the mere voice of Love Himself stirred his decaying heart to beat, and the stinking man sat up. Jesus didn't shrink back from the cosmic sign but said, "I am the resurrection and the life" (John 11:1-45).

Because when one young boy brought five mere broken loaves, his little lunch fed the bellies of the famished five thousand. That boy could take the witness stand when Jesus testified to a whole world of cravings, "I am the bread of life" (John 6:35).

Because when the blind man who lived in a world of thick pitch-dark, who felt the warmth of the saliva of God smeared with gritty soil across his eyes, felt the scales fall off, he about split as he felt the radiant full color of Jesus' words: "I am the light of the world" (John 8:12; 9:5).

The seven great "I Am" statements of Christ recorded by the pen of John are underlined by the seven signs of Christ—from the miraculous turning of water into rich wine to the healing of the fevered son of the brazenly faithful official to the heels of the Son of God finding the solidity of a highway on waves.

All the signs of Jesus point to the cruciform love of Christ, and all the words of Jesus boldly proclaim the deity and very identity of Christ. The signs may point to who Jesus is, but Jesus clearly points out to anyone willing to listen who He really is. Jesus boldly states that He is not just loving; He is Love. He is not a sign pointing to true things; He is the Truth. He is not just one way; He is the Way. He is not just life-giving; He is Life.

John was saying right from the beginning, "In him was life" (John 1:4). And John couldn't stop underlining that Jesus is the only lifeline to real life: "God gave us eternal life, and this life is in his Son. Whoever has the Son has life; whoever does not have the Son of God does not have life" (1 John 5:11-12, ESV). Stay in Him, and you stay alive. Leave Him, and you leave living. The Life came so you could really live: "I came that they may have life and have it abundantly" (John 10:10, ESV). If you stay in Jesus and invite Jesus to dwell in you, real life is in you, and you are in real life. Your life will now never end: "I give them eternal life, and they will never perish" (John 10:28, ESV).

Union with Jesus, who is Life, is the only way to have life.

Jesus is Life, the heart where your life finds its beat, the arteries that pump hope into your veins, the lungs that breathe you into who you are meant to be, and the hand that moves you closer to connecting intimacy.

The love and passion of Jesus wants all your love and passions.

And the destination every pilgrimage is moving toward is connection. The destination we all seek is intimacy.

And Jesus is the Way—the way for you to experience the intimacy, passion, presence, paradise, and the Promised Land of God. Jesus is the only way to move you from knowing God only as lawgiver to also knowing Him as Lover. Jesus is the only way to turn you from knowing God as merely angry with you to knowing Him as ardent for you, from believing He's only disappointed with you to accepting that He's relentlessly delighting in you. See the caress of Jesus' hand, and you see the compassion of God. Watch Jesus kneel low to tenderly tilt a shamed woman's chin, and you see how the heart of God is tilted toward yours. Jesus, the Word in flesh, narrates the heart of God. Because Jesus *is* God. God is not some abusive Father who nails His Son with His anger. Jesus is God who nails down His committed love to you forever through the suffering passion of His Son. Jesus isn't merely a learned man, logically explaining the meaning of life; He is the singular logos of the world (John 1:1), the Word who is the sole logic of the meaning of all of life. Your senseless messes find meaning in Him, your hidden wreckage finds hopeful resurrection in Him, and every single one of your trials and heartbreaks discover deepest meaning in Him.

You have heard it said, "Tell your truth, live your truth," but Jesus is the only Truth in all the universe who has arms to hold you, who has a heart that beats strong enough, close enough, to revive yours, who has eyes to gently find yours and reach out with nail-scarred hands to wipe every tear with tender hope. All other truth is wholly abstraction. Only Jesus is the Truth who is holy affection.

Absolute truth is actually a Person—a Person who absolutely loves you and can't *not* love you, because He is Love.

What lesser loves might you let go of to fall into a deeper love with Him?

King Jesus told His friends He would be going away, but He was the Way making the way, the Lord of heaven and earth, departing to heaven so He could design a dwelling place beyond anything your eye has ever seen or your heart could ever imagine. What more can you ask for when you know that He's coming back for you?

You can feel all your anxiety calm: You don't have to know the route— you only need to know the Way Himself. You don't need a map for life; you get Jesus, who is the Life and the Way.

Your held heart feels His gentle caress. "Follow thou Me. I am the way and the truth and the life. Without the way there is no going; without the truth there is no knowing; without the life there is no living. I am the way which thou must follow; the truth which thou must believe; the life for which thou must hope. I am the inviolable way; the infallible truth, the never-ending life. I am the straightest way; the sovereign truth; life true, life blessed, life uncreated," writes the ancient Thomas à Kempis, of the heart of Jesus.[3]

Jesus is the Life. Success isn't the life, accolade isn't the life, vacation isn't the life, romance isn't the life, family isn't the life, dazzle isn't the life, the dream isn't the life—*Jesus* is the Life.

Just need Jesus, and you have everything you need for the life you want.

PERSONAL NOTES TO SOUL FROM TODAY'S PILGRIMAGE INTO THE HEART OF JESUS:

_____

_____

_____

YOUR ADVOCATE

"If you love me, you will keep my commandments. And I will ask the Father, and he will give you another Helper, to be with you forever, even the Spirit of truth, whom the world cannot receive, because it neither sees him nor knows him. You know him, for he dwells with you and will be in you.

"I will not leave you as orphans; I will come to you. Yet a little while and the world will see me no more, but you will see me. Because I live, you also will live. In that day you will know that I am in my Father, and you in me, and I in you. Whoever has my commandments and keeps them, he it is who loves me. And he who loves me will be loved by my Father, and I will love him and manifest myself to him." Judas (not Iscariot) said to him, "Lord, how is it that you will manifest yourself to us, and not to the world?" Jesus answered him, "If anyone loves me, he will keep my word, and my Father will love him, and we will come to him and make our home with him. Whoever does not love me does not keep my words. And the word that you hear is not mine but the Father's who sent me.

"These things I have spoken to you while I am still with you. But the Helper, the Holy Spirit, whom the Father will send in my name, he will teach you all things and bring to your remembrance all that I have said

Day *27: "I will not leave you as orphans." John 14:18*

to you. Peace I leave with you; my peace I give to you. Not as the world gives do I give to you. Let not your hearts be troubled, neither let them be afraid."

JOHN 14:15-27, ESV

YOU'RE STANDING at the early-morning window, your hands wrapped around your first steaming mug, watching the sky lighten with hope, and you see some scene of an old sin-flash, feel how the accuser mocks, and it's your memory that burns.

Or you're up to your elbows in suds and crusty pans in the kitchen sink, and out of nowhere, you remember something you did that you're desperate to scrub clean.

Or your head hits the pillow, and you feel that cold hiss at the curve of your cochlea with the memory of some ugly failure you'd about die to fix.

And you feel it: Your failure to be utterly perfect never fails to utterly wreck you, and your conscience never stops morphing into a courtroom. And you grow weary of it: You are the accused.

But even now you feel the deep relief of it: You will never be without help. You will never have to find your own way through; you will never find yourself abandoned, because you have the God of the universe coming to you, coming for you, *because He is for you.*

Jesus had just held the heels of the disciples' grimy feet in the palm of His hand and embodied His sacrificial passion for each of them. And then He found their eyes. He finds your eyes too: "If you love me . . . keep my commandments."

Your eyes find His: How in the world can I do this? How do I keep loving Him enough to keep His Word? And how does this keep me on the way to the realest life?

The reality that few talk about is simply this: Loving without keeping His Word only keeps you in cheap emotionalism, and keeping His Word without love only keeps you enslaved to crushing legalism.

You feel it: A failure to keep His Word—the Word that keeps you in the fullest life—is actually a failure somewhere along the way to keep loving Him. And your heart cracks: There is no greater ache than the failure to love like you'd like to, because loving is living.

Loving is living.

And you can read the truth of it right there in His eyes: Keeping His Word is what reveals your love for Him—and it's your love for Him that keeps fueling you to keep His Word. This is the virtuous circle of fully living.

Only love that keeps His Word can keep saying it loves Him. And it is love for Him that unfurls realest life in us.

You can only keep keeping His Word if you keep stoking the heat of your passion for Him. This is the purpose of being.

Loving is living.

Your ardent passion for Jesus is what first moves you to live in accordance with His Word, which is what then moves you to deeply abide in Him, which is what then moves Him to move into *you.* The heart where love and obedience reside is where God moves in and makes His home.

But all this seems devastatingly impossible—and He knows.

While you are chosen to love Christ alone, above all else, you never undertake the daily work of loving Him alone. You are given more than just some help to love God—you are actually designated another full-time Helper who calls your heart home.

Nowhere else in the New Testament besides these three chapters of John is this word ever penned to describe helper as *paraklētos* except by the same pen of John in 1 John 2:1: "My little children, I am writing these things to you so that you may not sin. But if anyone does sin, we have an advocate with the Father, Jesus Christ the righteous" (ESV).

Jesus Himself is your first Paraclete, your Advocate who lives to advocate for you, intercede for you, and defend you. Advocating for you is now Jesus' full-time, 24–7 job, the one He never stops doing, the one His attention never wanes from, the one He never feels less passionate about.

The One who spoke the cosmos into its song across space became your Advocate—the One who speaks for you in the cosmic courtroom. The

One who made the mountains stand as a fence at the coastal edge of land is now the One who stands for you as your protective defense before the cosmic Judge. The One who holds whole crashing oceans in the palms of His hands also holds back any condemnation against you with nail-scarred hands that are inscribed with the very letters of your name.

What is of paramount importance is this: Jesus' advocacy for you isn't merely appealing to His sympathy; His advocacy for you appeals to divine justice. Yes, you failed again, but yes, *He has already paid the price in full.* You aren't alone in any tangled mess of life. You may fail again and again, but your Advocate relentlessly points, again and again, to the law that has already been satisfied and fulfilled through His sacrifice for you. Your prosecutor can point to your failings as many times as he wants, yet your Advocate points more times than you can imagine to your name etched in His nail-scarred hands. He points to how His passion for you drove Him to the Cross to die in your place so that by the law, the Judge *has to* let you go free, with *absolutely no condemnation.* You are fully acquitted of everything you've ever done wrong—not because your Advocate got you off, but because your Advocate took you on, and took on all your condemnation, and His passionate love for you never quits.

Anyone who has ever been on trial knows it, can testify to it, and it changes everything: Through every one of your trials, your Advocate is your whole world. The One who stands in your defense becomes your whole identity. His wisdom is seen as yours, His logic is seen as yours, His rightness is seen as yours, His absolute perfection is seen as yours. And your heart becomes His. *Forever.*

Once Jesus is your Advocate, your peace is *absolute.* Once Jesus is your Advocate, your standing is *assured.* Once Jesus is your Advocate, you're forever *approved.* And His passion for you ignites your passion for Him.

Loving is living.

Your Advocate is more than a good lawyer; your Advocate is perfect Love Himself, who fulfills the law for you—and then *asks to be with you forever.* When you see how Jesus represents you, everyone sees how His presence is your most cherished gift.

Jesus so wants you to never be abandoned, but to always have an

Advocate that He gives you, yet another Paraclete and Helper, a personal presence with you who is a comforter, a counselor, a consoler, a strengthener, an encourager—a *second* Advocate. This second Paraclete—literally meaning one beside you who is calling, speaking—isn't a drill sergeant barking orders from behind you or a head coach snapping calls ahead of you. Rather, the Paraclete is another advocate who comes alongside you and speaks up for you because He's for you.

Though the devil may be your daily accuser, you have the Spirit as your very own divine, daily Helper. And when the Holy Spirit abides in you, how can you be anything but awed by His holy power through you? With the Spirit with you, with the Spirit in you, with the Spirit for you, there is now no distance between God and you.

That is worth long dwelling on: All distance between us and God is now *decimated* because very God *dwells in us.*

This One who is your second Advocate, the Holy Spirit, is like a floodlight for you, so you are never left alone to stumble through the dark. "When floodlighting is well done, the floodlights are so placed that you do not see them; you are not in fact supposed to see where the light is coming from; what you are meant to see is just the building on which the floodlights are trained," writes J. I. Packer. "This perfectly illustrates the Spirit's new covenant role. He is, so to speak, the hidden floodlight shining on the Saviour. . . . The Spirit, we might say, is the matchmaker, the celestial marriage broker, whose role it is to bring us and Christ together and ensure that we stay together."[1]

The second Advocate is a floodlight in your life, shining on the first Advocate, and that is how you know the Spirit is within you: Because *everything* in your life is now about Him. Your heart becomes His, passionately fused to Christ, who moves into you to make you His residence for always.

Loving is living. And your home, *your life*, is where His heart is.

And when God moves in to make His home in you, trouble can't move you, because God Himself fills your doorways, God Himself keeps the midnight oil burning to keep watch over you, and God Himself keeps stoking the hearth of your heart with more of Himself.

How can your heart be troubled when God makes His full-time

residence in your heart? You may have trouble in your day but no trouble that can truly ruin your day. When Love Himself moves into the anxious rooms of your heart, there's no room for hopelessness, because His love is our sure and certain hope.

You don't face the unknown, the questions, the impossibles, the accuser, the failures, the future alone—you face the face of God, and you get an Advocate who brings a peace that's ironclad, a peace strengthened with the nails of the Cross, a peace that defends you and covers you because the nail-scarred, ardent Advocate won't let any prosecuting accusation ever touch you, because He alone holds you. When you say yes to the Advocate's defensive lawyering and divine love, He moves in with a perfect peace that renovates every space within you, and you can feel it.

You get the spaciousness of the shared life; you get real union and communion and oneness with Him. *Loving is living.*

Every moment, Love Himself moves you, in your pilgrimage toward Home and Him—and every single moment, the reality is: You are already the home of God.

PERSONAL NOTES TO SOUL FROM TODAY'S PILGRIMAGE INTO THE HEART OF JESUS:

HOW CAN
YOUR HEART
BE TROUBLED
WHEN GOD
MAKES HIS
FULL-TIME
RESIDENCE
IN YOUR
HEART?

ABIDE

"I am the true vine, and my Father is the gardener. He cuts off every branch in me that bears no fruit, while every branch that does bear fruit he prunes so that it will be even more fruitful. You are already clean because of the word I have spoken to you. Remain in me, as I also remain in you. No branch can bear fruit by itself; it must remain in the vine. Neither can you bear fruit unless you remain in me.

"I am the vine; you are the branches. If you remain in me and I in you, you will bear much fruit; apart from me you can do nothing. . . .

". . . My command is this: Love each other as I have loved you. Greater love has no one than this: to lay down one's life for one's friends. You are my friends if you do what I command. I no longer call you servants, because a servant does not know his master's business. Instead, I have called you friends, for everything that I learned from my Father I have made known to you. You did not choose me, but I chose you and appointed you so that you might go and bear fruit—fruit that will last—and so that whatever you ask in my name the Father will give you. This is my command: Love each other."

JOHN 15:1-5, 12-17

Day *28: "I am the true vine." John 15:1*

YOU AREN'T MOST KNOWN as the one who failed or the one who struggles the most. You aren't identified as the one who's liked the least, the one who's merely tolerated, the one who missed out, the one who got it all wrong, the one who got filed on a shelf, the one who got the pink slip. You aren't the one left on the sidelines, left behind, left ashamed; you aren't the one who isn't enough, isn't included, isn't remembered. You aren't the one who is X, Y, or whatever terrible Z you whisper to yourself at 3:00 a.m.

Whatever happened doesn't define who you happen to be.

The most definite thing about you is that you are the one whom Jesus definitely loves.

The truest, most abiding thing about you is that Love Himself, Jesus Himself, loves you and truly abides in you.

And what God says about your identity is *who you are* in reality.

Your identity isn't based on what you think of yourself, or on what anyone else thinks of you—your identity is based on the belovedness that God actually sings over you (Zephaniah 3:17).

In the midst of the heartbreaks and failures, the only way through is to picture yourself as a vulnerable lamb abiding in the arms of Jesus—and let the triune God Himself do everything through you, carrying you through.

To abide in God is to live in God. His arms are your home, His heartbeat regulates yours, His body is your soul protection.

Confounding as that word *abide* is—used nearly three times less frequently now than in the 1800s—theologians actually consider it to be one of the most important words in the whole Bible. The whole of the Christ-life is *wholly about abiding*. As the lamb abides in the arms of the Good Shepherd, as the branch abides in the fruitful vine, the soul abides in the life of God.

As the lamb is attached to the shepherd, as the branch is attached to the vine—to abide in God is to be *attached* to God.

As the theologian Andrew Murray writes, "During the life of Jesus on earth, the word He chiefly used when speaking of the relations of the disciples to Himself was: 'Follow me.' When about to leave for heaven, He gave them a new word, to express their more intimate and spiritual union.

That chosen word was: 'Abide in Me.'"[1] *Abide* comes from the English word prefix *a-*, meaning "onward," and *bidan*, which means "to remain or stay."

You move onward, while you stay in Jesus.

You continue on, by continuing to remain in Jesus.

You only pilgrimage into the realest life by *remaining in Jesus* every moment of your life.

In Greek, the word for *abide* is *menó*, and it means "to remain, to reside, to take up permanent residence" or "to make yourself at home."

To abide in Christ is to be most at home with Christ. Which means your soul is most at home with Him; your loves and passions and desires and longings and comfort are all most at home in Jesus.

The atonement at the Cross was for Christ's at-home-ness with you.

To abide in Christ means nothing less than to reside fully in Christ. Which is to say: Jesus is our passion, Jesus is our person, Jesus is our primary residence. Jesus only moves from an abstract idea to our lived reality when we move our lives into Him to abide in Him, reside in Him.

Because the healthiest people live in the arms of Jesus. Like the lamb moves with the shepherd, lives in the shadow of the shepherd's every step, lives in the safe arms of the shepherd's care, to abide in Christ is to be of one mind with Christ, to put before our eyes what Christ would put before His, to listen to what He would listen to, read what He would read. To abide in Christ is to have unbroken communion with Christ.

It turns out: You can go about looking like a Christian and not actually be abiding in Christ. You can go to church and not be one with Christ. You can open the Word and not be one with the Word. You can be connected to a life of faith and not be one with Life Himself. Only when you live and move and have your whole being in Him can you *wholly live.*

You have no life apart from the vine. The branch is absolutely dead unless it's attached to the vine. Your life isn't the vine of your accolades; your life isn't the vine of your comfort, your accomplishments, your relationships, your family, your health, your plans, or your expectations—the vine of your life is Jesus. *Jesus is the Life.*

Attachment to Jesus is life.

When the vine of your life is Jesus, nothing can steal your joy, your fruit, or your flourishing.

The most definite thing about you is that you are the one whom Jesus *definitely* loves. Move in with Him, and only move in Him, and watch how He moves life and fruit through you. There is no *abundant* life apart from consciously *abiding* in Christ. Abiding in Christ always leads to abundant fruit in our lives, and it's only being full of Christ that can ever make life fruitful. What is most vital for a life of vitality is union with Christ.

You can't live a good life—you will need the One who *is* good to live His life through you.

Ultimate *happiness* is actually genuine *fruitfulness*.

It's actually a relief: You don't have to muster up the fruit, or stress over the production of the fruit, or duct-tape on some fake fruit. You have one job and one job only: All you have to do is abide in Christ, be most at home in Christ, surrender all other residences, and make Christ your primary residence. You don't need a self-help book, you don't need some five-step plan—you simply need to abide in the vine. Abide in the Shepherd, abide in the vine—and the Gardener alone will produce the abundant fruit, the Shepherd alone will protect your life. The Shepherd does all the work. The Gardener does all the work. All your work is simply the work of resting, remaining in Him, staying in Him, being most at home in Him.

Jesus would never ask you to do the work of abiding in Him if He weren't first abiding in you, doing all the work. All the work ahead of you is always simply the work of Jesus within you. You can only abide in God and be at home in Him because God abides in you and is already at home *within you.*

"The Christian way is different: harder, and easier," writes C. S. Lewis. "Christ says, 'Give me All. I don't want so much of your time and so much of your money and so much of your work: I want You. I have not come to torment your natural self, but to kill it. No half-measures are any good. I don't want to cut off a branch here and a branch there, I want to have the whole tree down. . . . Hand over the whole natural self, all the desires which you think innocent as well as the ones you think wicked—the whole outfit. I will give you a new self instead. In fact, I will give you Myself: my own shall become yours.'"[2]

And your heart moves close to His and you offer: "I surrender. I hand over all my old passions. Give me a new heart. Please give me Yourself. And let Your passionate, sacrificial love for me become my passionate, sacrificial love for You. Your life given—to give me life. You are loving me to life."

To become a Christian is nothing less than to come into the life of the Vine and say to Jesus, "You are mine. You are my life, You are my thoughts, You are my actions, You are my decisions, You are my movement. You are in me and I am in You, and our shared life is the most fulfilling, passionate life." When you live in the Vine, the divine life has entered you. Abide in the Vine, and the divine life flows from you.

And never doubt: There is a staggering difference between the life of a Jesus-striver and the life of a Jesus-abider.

Striving for Jesus can be done in your own strength.

Abiding in Jesus means He is your *only* strength.

Striving for Jesus means you keep striving forward in and of yourself. Abiding in Jesus keeps you from backsliding because you are *in Him*.

Striving for Jesus means you can go wayward because the best you can do is *think about* God.

Abiding in Jesus is obeying God because now you are thinking with God, *living in* God.

Abiding always gives the grace to obey. Obedience to God can only flow out of oneness with God.

Thinking about God may change your thoughts, but only abiding with God, in God, is thinking with God, moving with God—and *this* is what changes your heart, changes your actions. *Abiding* in His arms, residing in His arms, is the way your hands, feet, and heart live in *obedience* to Him. As you abide in Jesus, obeying the Word, so Jesus abides in you, giving you grace to *live* the Word.

You don't have to fight anymore, you don't have to fear anymore, you don't have to try to be enough anymore. Move into Jesus' arms, and He moves through you. Abiding holds you in His embrace of grace, and abiding holds the key to obeying.

That is all there is to the pilgrimage of really living. Every day there's only one thing that is needed to truly flourish and fully live: Be one with God.

Be relieved: No matter what you think might not bode well in your life, all is always well when you simply abide in God.

Be at peace: No matter what, you are the disciple Jesus definitely loves, the one He is loving to life. And this is the pilgrimage of every moment: Abide in the abode of God.

ALL IS

ALWAYS WELL

WHEN YOU

HUMBLY ABIDE

IN GOD.

OUT OF THIS WORLD

"If the world hates you, know that it has hated me before it hated you. If you were of the world, the world would love you as its own; but because you are not of the world, but I chose you out of the world, therefore the world hates you. Remember the word that I said to you: 'A servant is not greater than his master.' If they persecuted me, they will also persecute you. If they kept my word, they will also keep yours. But all these things they will do to you on account of my name, because they do not know him who sent me. . . .

"But when the Helper comes, whom I will send to you from the Father, the Spirit of truth, who proceeds from the Father, he will bear witness about me. And you also will bear witness, because you have been with me from the beginning."

JOHN 15:18-21, 26-27, ESV

Day *29*: *"You are not of the world." John 15:19*

Chosen out of this world.

Hand-selected out of this world by the Maker of heaven and earth to be a citizen, not of this world, but of heaven. This moves you out of this world and makes you an insider with the King of the universe.

Your heart and mind keep returning to this address: *This world is not my home; I abide in the abode of God.*

And Jesus tenderly traces your scars. Your allegiance to Jesus may antagonize some, and your passionate relationship with Him may cause others to passionately hate you. But Jesus loves you enough to gently tell you, to prepare you: When you lean up against Jesus, the world is going to be against you. When you make otherworldly love your whole world, this world doesn't understand that kind of love and may hate you for it. This is a tender word; this is a hard word.

It was just after the Last Supper, just after Jesus' washing of the disciples' feet as an example of His dying and undying love that will never end. And now His Love lingered in the upper room, sharing parting words to prepare His friends—*and you*—for after He's gone.

The religious and pompous had been plotting Jesus' death since He beckoned rotting Lazarus to life (John 11:43), and they decreed that anyone following Jesus would be tossed out of the synagogue (John 9:22). Jesus knew it.

Seven times, Jesus said the world hates those who follow Him. But is it a surprise that those not grafted into the vine of Love Himself would yield all shades of hate? If you aren't grafted into Love, what you're actually growing is fear—and fear produces hostility, scarcity, animosity. If hate is in your heart, are you actually in Love Himself? And if your faith causes you to hate, then is it possible that yours isn't the faith of Love Himself? How can you hate anyone when Jesus loved them so much that He loved them to death and back to the fullest life again?

Conversely, when you're grafted into the vine of Love Himself, there's the abundant fruit of humility, generosity, cruciformity. *Genuine* love is always the genuine fruit of those who abide in the vine of Love Himself.

Jesus finds your eyes, His heart searching yours: If you commit to following a persecuted Savior and you aren't being persecuted, are you truly following Him?

It's Jesus' least-liked promise: Three times in the upper room, Jesus promised that if you truly follow Him, you will truly know persecution. When you follow a way of exclusivity, you can expect much animosity on the way. But this is the way of Jesus: "Blessed are those who are persecuted because of righteousness, for theirs is the kingdom of heaven. Blessed are you when people insult you, persecute you and falsely say all kinds of evil against you because of me. Rejoice and be glad, because great is your reward in heaven, for in the same way they persecuted the prophets who were before you" (Matthew 5:10-12).

The kingdoms of the world live a profoundly different trajectory than the upside-down Kingdom of God, with its cruciform way of peace, its cruciform way of nonviolence, its cruciform way of self-sacrifice, its cruciform way of laying down your life. This cruciform way isn't the way of the power-hungry, both within the church and outside of it. But it is always the way King Jesus is lifted high.

Those who are passionate about Jesus, who long to live a truly passionate life, will always be a persecuted people. The literal definition of passion is to suffer. *There is no way to live a passionate life without suffering.*

Jesus reaches out to find your hand. Feel the depth of His scars? Jesus wasn't hated because He grasped for authoritative power; Jesus was hated because He surrendered His authority to the authority of God alone. Sometimes people reject those whose lives convict them about their own.

Jesus wasn't hated because He was obscenely wealthy; Jesus was hated because He loved obscenely. Sometimes people reject those whose rich compassion exposes their own poverty of compassion.

Jesus wasn't hated because He looked out for His own interests; Jesus was hated because He laid down His life to protect the interests of other people. Sometimes people reject those whose selfless sacrifice lays bare their own self-protection and smallness of heart.

If you're truly on pilgrimage, following the way Jesus lives, and the world rejected Him for His way—are you living and loving so much like Him that they reject you in certain ways too?

Why would a follower of Jesus want to be treated any better than Jesus? What greater gift could there be than to be treated like the One you follow?

Instead of being rejected because we arrogantly mock anyone as foolish, we could be rejected for the foolishness of our lavish love.

Instead of being rejected because we take sides or because we create greater margins of power for ourselves, we could be sidelined for how we radically lay down our lives for the marginalized.

Instead of being rejected because we refuse to pick up a cross at any point in our lives, we could be unpopular because of our cruciform compassion that loves others to life.

If we long to be the hands and feet of Jesus in the world, can we embrace what happened to Jesus' hands and feet?

PERSONAL NOTES TO SOUL FROM TODAY'S PILGRIMAGE INTO THE HEART OF JESUS:

THIS WORLD

IS NOT MY HOME;

I ABIDE IN

THE ABODE

OF GOD.

AN
UNTROUBLED HEART

"I have said these things to you in figures of speech. The hour is coming when I will no longer speak to you in figures of speech but will tell you plainly about the Father. In that day you will ask in my name, and I do not say to you that I will ask the Father on your behalf; for the Father himself loves you, because you have loved me and have believed that I came from God. I came from the Father and have come into the world, and now I am leaving the world and going to the Father."

His disciples said, "Ah, now you are speaking plainly and not using figurative speech! Now we know that you know all things and do not need anyone to question you; this is why we believe that you came from God." Jesus answered them, "Do you now believe? Behold, the hour is coming, indeed it has come, when you will be scattered, each to his own home, and will leave me alone. Yet I am not alone, for the Father is with me. I have said these things to you, that in me you may have peace. In the world you will have tribulation. But take heart; I have overcome the world."

JOHN 16:25-33, ESV

Day 30: *"Take heart; I have overcome the world." John 16:33*

YOU'VE GOT TO KNOW—no one twisted God's arm to get Him to love you. He gave His whole heart because He *likes* you, because He *wants* to be with you. This may be the hardest to believe, but it's truer than your next breath.

In Jesus' last hours, with only so much time left to say all that He wanted His friends to know before He left, He summed up everything He'd said and gave you the bottom line: The heart that beats at the center of the universe is passionate about your heart.

You don't want to miss this.

"For the Father himself loves you, because you have loved me . . ."

The Father Himself has never stopped being passionate about you, His very own child. God doesn't for a moment begrudge calling you His beloved. God isn't a furious father whose Son begged and cajoled Him into putting up with you, tolerating you. There was no one persuading and prodding God to meet you with grace—grace has always been His very heartbeat for you. "Jesus makes it clear that the Son did not need to persuade an angry Father to be gracious; but His work would provide a righteous basis for God's graciousness. [Jesus] did not die to change God into love; he died to tell us that God is love. He came, not because God so hated the world, but because he so *loved* the world."[1]

Your passionate love for Jesus is actually proof of God's love first for you—proof that His love for you *first* is what moves you to love *at all*. You can't miss the miracle of this.

Just like it's not your pulse that keeps your arteries pumping, but rather your pulse that's proof that your heart is actually pumping, your ardency for God isn't what makes God love you; rather, your love for Him is *visible proof* of His love—which only stirs your own heart's love even more for Him. This is *everything*.

Can you believe that Love Himself came down from the heart of God because your heart was so tender, so broken by our broken world, that God couldn't merely send down some good morals and standards and principles to live by? He had to *personally* come as a Messiah to meet the standard, save us from death, and love us back to the very fullest life.

Jesus came from the Father's heart, so your heart would be profoundly and forever touched by the Father's heart for *you*.

When your heart starts to worry about all the things, pull your heart close and comfort it: Nothing in the future can ever stop the love of God from coming to protect you. Worry is a distrust of the love of God. Surrender to the relief of peace, and trust that every moment in the future will have more than enough of the love of God.

You can feel the deep peace of God hold you when you simply let the passionate love of God fully embrace you, especially right here and now.

Christ knows what you ultimately want, what you desperately seek: the completeness of peace. Which is to say, you long for the lack of lack. The wholeness of shalom. And when you abide in the abode of the love of God, shalom becomes your home. You can have this; you are fully welcomed and ushered into all this peace right now.

To know yourself deeply is to know the depths of your need—against the measure of Truth—and yet still feel real peace, because you know the unconditional, unwavering love of Love Himself.

It's only when we first see the Love who Jesus is that we can see the way to live. Christianity is intimacy before it is ideology. When you rightly see the heart of Jesus for you, you begin to rightly see the way of peace through everything.

And in one sentence, Jesus speaks the four deepest truths to you about who He is:

He is divine love; He came from God in heaven: "I came from the Father."

He is human hope; He was incarnated here on earth: "I . . . entered the world."

He is saving atonement, to give you at-one-ment with God; He passionately and voluntarily took your stead on the Cross: "I am leaving the world."

He is relentless protection, as He's interceding for you now; He lives to love you to life by relentlessly advocating nonstop for you: "I am . . . going back to the Father," because "He is able to save completely those who come to God through him, because he always lives to intercede for them" (Hebrews 7:25).

What deep pain could ever separate you from deep peace when you are loved to life with the deepest passion? Whatever you fear in the future, His love will not fail, His love cannot stop, His love does not end. Comfort your heart: Because His love is endless, so is your peace.

This is all so surreal, but it is real. This is a passionate love that seems unbelievable, but it's more believable than the next breath in your lungs. This out-of-this-world story is an otherworldly story—and the truest story. The greatest truth brings the greatest peace.

You have to know this, because this is why Jesus said everything, why He lingered in the upper room in the final hours before He laid down His life on the Cross *for you*. These were His final parting words—words He needs you to know: "I have said these things to you, that in me you may have peace."

Nowhere else in all the universe but in Christ may you know peace.

Peace is always a possibility, but that doesn't mean it's always practiced. Peace is promised to you, but it's your choice to practice it—by abiding in the person of Christ. Peace isn't found in circumstances, or because of circumstances, or through circumstances; peace is found only in Christ, because of Christ, through Christ. Peace isn't found when life is finally tied up with a bow; peace is found in the only One who nailed down His passion for you on a cross.

This changes everything: Your peace isn't about getting out of crisis; your peace is about staying in Christ.

Comfort your heart: You will have troubles. You have troubles coming right this moment, and they will not always be small troubles, but you have a large God with an incomprehensibly large love. And when you surrender to trust in His love through the troubles, this is what actually expands and enlarges your own soul.

In this world you will have tribulation. But take heart—take *His* heart to steady your heart. In Greek, "take heart" is *tharseó*, which means "to dare."

Dare to passionately and wholeheartedly live it: You can have troubles, but you can have an untroubled heart.

Dare to live it: No conditions in your life get to control the conditions of your heart.

Dare to believe your reality right now: Whatever troubles are agitating around you, they aren't the whole truth. The whole truth is that all your tribulations can't overshadow, overcome, or overwhelm Christ's affection for you, Christ's protection of you, or Christ's perfection in you.

When you know the truth—that you are fully known by the Truth Himself, and that He knows the deepest truths about you, and that He knows what's best and good and right, and that He carries all that truth in a heart of endless love for you—how can you feel anything but deep peace? *Breathe deeply, and fully live.*

No matter what trouble is coming, surrender and trust that Jesus will overcome it. And if it doesn't yet look like that, you just haven't yet come to the end of the story.

Dare to take the pilgrimage that takes heart in His heart that's always and only ever for you.

PERSONAL NOTES TO SOUL FROM TODAY'S PILGRIMAGE INTO THE HEART OF JESUS:

THE SAME PASSION

"My prayer is not for them alone. I pray also for those who will believe in me through their message, that all of them may be one, Father, just as you are in me and I am in you. May they also be in us so that the world may believe that you have sent me. I have given them the glory that you gave me, that they may be one as we are one— I in them and you in me—so that they may be brought to complete unity. Then the world will know that you sent me and have loved them even as you have loved me.

"Father, I want those you have given me to be with me where I am, and to see my glory, the glory you have given me because you loved me before the creation of the world.

"Righteous Father, though the world does not know you, I know you, and they know that you have sent me. I have made you known to them, and will continue to make you known in order that the love you have for me may be in them and that I myself may be in them."

JOHN 17:20-26

Day 31: "I pray . . . that all of them may be one." John 17:20-21

YOUR NAME LIVES on the lips of the King of the universe, and His heart cry, just before His death, was for your heart. When you know that in His final hours, Jesus' deepest desire was for you to be safe in His love, that His heart cry was turned to you, that He poured out His heart in prayer for you, interceding and advocating across all the ages and history *specifically for you*—how does your soul not expand and unite with the Love who is Christ?

In His final hours after the Last Supper, just before His crucifixion, as He lingered in the upper room with His disciples, speaking His final words on earth, Jesus prayed *literally for you*: "I pray also for those who will believe in me . . ."

The One who brought you into existence is carrying you in prayer when that existence is brutally hard.

What could matter more?

Jesus "always lives to make intercession for [you]" (Hebrews 7:25, ESV).

Jesus has set aside all of forever to pray that you will be set apart for the realest life right now.

The One who breathed the stars into existence breathes prayers for you; the One whose words spoke the world into being uses priceless words over your being; the One who made time, lives beyond time, controls all of time, uses all of His time to pray for you—because you are priceless to Him.

Jesus is praying right now that the Spirit will comfort you, strengthen you, anoint you with the fresh oil of brave joy. Right this very moment, Jesus is praying that you'll be brave when you're about to break, that you'll turn from what's tempting, that you'll stand against what's strangling, that you'll escape into Him instead of trying to escape in a thousand unfulfilling ways.

Hard times don't need to understand what God's doing like they need to know God's standing with us, that He's kneeling in prayer for us at all times. Nothing makes you more fiercely brave than knowing Jesus is fiercely praying for you.

We can get through anything because Jesus is seeing us through, carrying us through, praying us through. And when we're struggling to pray, it's Jesus Himself who prays for all we're struggling with.

There are arms that won't let you go, there are plans that won't abandon you, there are prayers that won't fail you. *The hand of God finds yours.*

Prayer is the aching hope of the heart, the cry at the core, the opening of the hands to place it all in God's hands. Prayer is "something great, supernatural, which expands [the] soul and unites [us] to Jesus," writes Thérèse of Lisieux.[1]

Frederick Christian Bauerschmidt writes that Jesus' "whole life is a prayer because it is the . . . eternal conversation of love that is the life of God as Father, Son, and Holy Spirit."[2] Your name is part of the eternal, endless conversation of love between God the Father, God the Son, and God the Holy Spirit.

The moment you believe in Jesus, you live always in Jesus' prayers.

In every one of your crises, you get to do more than merely find shelter—you get to shelter in God. Prayer is a soul-mover, moving you into the presence of Love, who is Jesus.

How do you know if you could find yourself in the very life of God, which is perfect love? Your Love Himself prays to Abba Father about you, for you: "The world will know that you sent me and have loved them even as you have loved me."

What love could be more lavish and extravagant in all the cosmos? You're intimately enveloped in the very same perfect, endless, all-encompassing love that God intimately shares with Jesus.

As R. T. Kendall, pastor of the historic Westminster Chapel in London, writes, "There is . . . dazzling truth, and that is that God loves you as much as He loves Jesus. Have you any idea how much God loves Jesus? Have you any idea how God feels about His one and only Son? The voice that came from heaven at Jesus' baptism said, 'You are my Son, whom I love; with you I am well pleased' (Mark 1:11). . . . [As] Romans 8:17 says, 'We are . . . co-heirs with Christ.' That means God loves us as much as He loves Jesus."[3]

In the same way that the God of the whole universe loves Jesus, the only perfect Person in the whole universe, God wholly loves *you*. This is at the heart of everything you ever need to know.

As the Father could not hardly or partly love His Son, so in Christ He could not barely or rarely love you. You are not hardly tolerated; you are *wholeheartedly loved*!

Can you even dare to whisper it? *The love God has for Jesus is the same love He has for me.*

The same, the same, the same! Let this love touch every part of you.

All your internal dialogue changes when your heart curves like an ear to hear God's eternal dialogue of love.

The greatest, fullest kind of love is more than a love that gives; it is a love that is humble enough to open up and receive, so everything tender within can be healed.

"If the Father is in him, and he is in them, then the Father is in them: they are drawn into the very life of God, and the life of God is perfect love," writes F. F. Bruce.[4]

The love within the Trinity is the endless, the self-giving love of the Father, sacrificially given to the Son, who passionately gives to the Spirit, who lovingly serves all.

You can see what Augustine described: "If you see love, you see the Trinity."[5]

This last prayer of Jesus takes us into the very heartbeat of the mission and ministry of Jesus. This proves what is at the very pulse of the fullest life that is the Christ-life: sacrificial, passionate love.

In a fragmented world, with all the shards of broken hearts, Jesus' passion for you stirred Him to pray that all His followers would be united to one another in love and united to Him. He prayed that we would abide in the love of the Lamb of God, "that all of them may be one, Father, just as you are in me and I am in you. May they also be in us."

The validity of Jesus' ministry is appraised on, and praised for, your loving unity. Which means that when you don't pursue loving unity, you are defying one of the very tenets of Jesus' ministry. This begs reflection. Because when Love Himself indwells you, you are loved to life, *to live a life of love*. Sacrificial, passionate love will always cost you something. It is always impartially for everyone, and offers forgiveness at any time, trusting that forgiving love can still be cruciform, boundaried love.

It's a tender and hopeful truth: Because of the genuine love of Christ, there is possibility for genuine community.

And when you live the very real, sacrificial, passionate love of Christ in community, the doubts against the very reality of Christ are quieted because of overwhelming love.

At the center, God's name is Love, and Jesus declared it, proclaimed it, lived it. As Jesus prepared to pour out God's whole passion on the Cross, the whole of Jesus' life was sustained and held and infused by His Father's passion for Him. Sustained by Love, He was about to save the world with love, because of love, to love us into the most expansive life.

And Jesus' final, great prayer, which could have been a prayer for a whole world of other things, was that nothing less than the same passionate love of God would now fuel and fill us to pilgrimage out into the world with His otherworldly love. Jesus endlessly lives to relentlessly pray this for you (Hebrews 7:25), and right this moment, He's praying for your protection, your interconnection, your God-satisfaction, and your always-sanctification (John 17:11-19).

Prayer is the pilgrimage. And when you just want Him, you always get just what you want.

PERSONAL NOTES TO SOUL FROM TODAY'S PILGRIMAGE INTO THE HEART OF JESUS:

_____

_____

_____

_____

_____

GO TO GOD

When Jesus had spoken these words, he went out with his disciples across the brook Kidron, where there was a garden, which he and his disciples entered. Now Judas, who betrayed him, also knew the place, for Jesus often met there with his disciples. So Judas, having procured a band of soldiers and some officers from the chief priests and the Pharisees, went there with lanterns and torches and weapons. Then Jesus, knowing all that would happen to him, came forward and said to them, "Whom do you seek?" They answered him, "Jesus of Nazareth." Jesus said to them, "I am he." Judas, who betrayed him, was standing with them. When Jesus said to them, "I am he," they drew back and fell to the ground. So he asked them again, "Whom do you seek?" And they said, "Jesus of Nazareth." Jesus answered, "I told you that I am he. So, if you seek me, let these men go." This was to fulfill the word that he had spoken: "Of those whom you gave me I have lost not one." Then Simon Peter, having a sword, drew it and struck the high priest's servant and cut off his right ear. (The servant's name was Malchus.) So Jesus said to Peter, "Put your sword into its sheath; shall I not drink the cup that the Father has given me?"

JOHN 18:1-11, ESV

Day *32*: *"Whom do you seek?" John 18:4*

WHERE IN THE WORLD do you go when the pressures of everything around you and within you are conspiring to take you down? When it's hard to swallow down the cup you've been given, when you find it hard to keep standing, to keep your feet on the ground, to not be flattened by life?

Jesus takes your hand and takes you where He was known to go. When life is falling apart all over the place, what your heart needs most is your own place of prayer.

Because always, the way to get perspective is to get away with God.

After the Passover meal in the upper room with His beloved friends, after sacramentally breaking bread with them, after embodying the broken and given life by bending low and sacrificially washing their feet, after praying for His followers to live a life of sacrificial, cruciform love, Jesus made His way through the darkening streets of Jerusalem one last time, crossing the Kidron Valley to enter into prayer and the Garden of Gethsemane.

Judas knew going to God was always the way of Jesus. This is always the way of Jesus; this is always the way to Life. Jesus did more than merely let go and let God; Jesus let go of everything else and *personally went to God*. Through a valley of deepest sorrow, sacrifice, and suffering, Jesus went to God. Is there really ever anywhere else to go? Pilgrimage into His presence, and no matter what happens, *you have arrived*.

As Jesus walked through the midnight pitch-dark of the Kidron Valley, He could hear the water from the floor of the Temple, which rose from the highest heights of Jerusalem, drain down into the Kidron Valley, mixed with the crimson blood of more than two hundred thousand slain Passover lambs, their lifeblood sprinkled on the Temple altar as the sacrifice for the broken and sinful hearts of more than two million of God's people.

The night air was thick, heavy with the scent of sacrifice. The Lamb of God knew He was about to sacrifice His own heart for the love of the world. The scent of love is always sacrifice.

Look into His eyes. How could He not, in that moment, in that valley soaked with lambs' blood, be remembering anything other than the to-die-for covenant He had made with Abram—with you—back in the beginning, when He had Abram split the bodies of sacrificed animals in half and let the parted animals' blood run like a stream, soaking a red valley across the earth (Genesis 15)? Jesus knew it: Ancient custom required that any two parties covenanted to each other must walk blood-soaked earth between sacrificed animals as a sign that whoever broke their promise of faithfulness would slit their own throats and let their own blood run.

Yet in the darkened shadows of that night more than one thousand years before, as the blood of the split animals had saturated the earth, Abram witnessed only a smoking pot and a burning torch—symbols of God in the cloud and flame—pass alone through the sacrificed animals.

Abram and all of us, his descendants, couldn't walk the blood-drenched earth and pass through the sacrificed and parted animals, because who can wholly keep their covenant of faithfulness to God?

But Jesus' heart wants nothing more than to be with you, so on the last night of His earthly life, He walked through the valley of death for you, to keep the whole covenant for you, to keep in close relationship with you. The passion of the Lamb of God moved Him to pass through the blood-stained valley for you.

Covenant kept.

Lamb laid down.

Passion poured out.

So we could be loved to life.

The passion of God made an "until death parts us" promise of forever commitment to you, so you could fully live forever. *He parts His own heart in half so He never has to be apart from your heart.* This love is what holds you when everything else is falling apart.

The One who went down into the Kidron Valley didn't have to be the Lamb who spilled His own life to wash away your deadness and brokenness and sinfulness to revive you to the realest life—*but He did.*

The One who went to the Garden didn't have to take the cup of unfathomable suffering to spare you—but He did.

You can be pilgrimaging down your own hard and narrow valley road, wondering why others have what seems like an easier road, a softer place to land, with all the lovely people and the picture-perfect life and all the large love you've always dreamed of, without any of the mangled, raised scars you bear, without the tangled, downtrodden way you're on, without any of the sacrifice that you've had to silently suffer.

But when you see how Jesus chose to take His cup of suffering for you, you can also take yours, the cup handed to you, and you can look to the sky and say, "You who have given me every breath, You don't owe me more. You who have given me one day, You don't owe me two. You who have given me every single heartbeat for every single second I have ever known, You don't owe me anything more."

Because the One who stood in the Garden before the hundreds of armed and torch-bearing Roman soldiers could have, with a word, terminated their confrontation.

Instead, He answered their search for Jesus of Nazareth by startlingly saying—no less than three times—that He was divine, the very I AM, with no beginning and no end: *I AM, I AM, I AM.*

Who can call Jesus merely a good teacher when He called Himself God, *to call you His*? No one can confine Jesus to being just some wise sage to dabble with, when He Himself claimed to be nothing less than the divine Savior to *dwell in*. He's either ultimately a swindler or the ultimate Savior. All other religions say we have to find God, but Jesus is very God come to earth, *come to find us*, because the only way to find God is to simply be still and receive the One who comes and finds you and keeps the whole covenant, *including the penalty*, to keep you.

You can see it: The moment that Jesus said, "I AM," hundreds of soldiers fell to the ground. Before Christ laid His life down on the Cross, He flattened everyone with His divinity. You can't encounter God and count on anything less than falling to your knees. *No one can truly face God and not fall on their face in true awe and gratitude.*

Awe makes us feel delightfully insignificant and significant, delightful joy. When we are awed, we feel smaller and part of something larger, which makes our joy larger. Awe makes us see that we—and our problems—are small and that one great God is over all. And when we feel smaller, we feel humility, which is the key to connectivity with God and people, the key to wholeness.

And come the final day, Judgment Day, who of us will be able to stand—stand on our own flawless performance, stand on our own impeccable laurels, stand on our perfectly faultless record? In the end, we will all be flattened with gratitude and awe in God.

Because the One who went to the Cross could have called down thousands of angels to free Himself, but He didn't. He chose to be our Lamb, to take the penalty of our broken covenant of faithfulness, to go to the Cross, to stay on that Cross for one purpose, and one purpose alone: to give His heart to you, to have your whole heart.

And then He gladly throws in infinitely more for you—like every sunrise coming with a whole sky full of fresh mercies, and the warmth of the sun on your face, and the next breath in your lungs, and all these seconds saturated with glory. At some point, you've got to ask, *How much life will ever be enough life? How much good will ever be enough good? How much God will ever be enough for us? How much more does the Lamb of God have to give, how much more does He have to sacrifice, how much does He have to lay down to ever be enough to satisfy my heart?*

If Jesus is actually the only One who ever loved us to death and then back to the realest and forever-and-ever life through His love, isn't life in this moment more than we could ever ask for? Life is either about how much we're owed by God or how much we're awed by God. Does God owe us more than choosing to be our very own slain Lamb? He drank the cup of unfathomable suffering—suffering He *chose* because He chooses *you*, chooses to pay for your soul-rescue with His crushed-down heart and wide-open arms. No amount of pain could ever stop His passionate love for you, because He sees value and worth in you. Jesus became your Lamb, who let His blood run to cover your sin, and Jesus took the cup of abandonment and death so you could drink the cup of communion and life.

So you can look up at the stars, even in the midst of your hard and winding pilgrimage, and be awed by God. The One who asks you to drink down your cup of ache with thanks—He drank down His far greater cup of ache, because His heart ached even more to hold you.

And you can always rest here in the pilgrimage: When God is your portion, you always have more than enough to whisper your awed thanks.

PERSONAL NOTES TO SOUL FROM TODAY'S PILGRIMAGE INTO THE HEART OF JESUS:

LIFE IS

EITHER ABOUT

HOW MUCH WE'RE

OWED BY GOD

OR HOW MUCH

WE'RE AWED

BY GOD.

FOREVER
BOUND TO YOU

Then the detachment of soldiers with its commander and the Jewish officials arrested Jesus. They bound him and brought him first to Annas, who was the father-in-law of Caiaphas, the high priest that year. Caiaphas was the one who had advised the Jewish leaders that it would be good if one man died for the people.

Simon Peter and another disciple were following Jesus. Because this disciple was known to the high priest, he went with Jesus into the high priest's courtyard, but Peter had to wait outside at the door. The other disciple, who was known to the high priest, came back, spoke to the servant girl on duty there and brought Peter in.

"You aren't one of this man's disciples too, are you?" she asked Peter. He replied, "I am not."

It was cold, and the servants and officials stood around a fire they had made to keep warm. Peter also was standing with them, warming himself.

Meanwhile, the high priest questioned Jesus about his disciples and his teaching.

"I have spoken openly to the world," Jesus replied. "I always taught in synagogues or at the temple, where all the Jews come together. I said nothing in secret. Why question me? Ask those who heard me. Surely they know what I said."

Day *33*: *"If I spoke the truth, why did you strike me?" John 18:23*

When Jesus said this, one of the officials nearby slapped him in the face. "Is this the way you answer the high priest?" he demanded.

"If I said something wrong," Jesus replied, "testify as to what is wrong. But if I spoke the truth, why did you strike me?" Then Annas sent him bound to Caiaphas the high priest.

JOHN 18:12-24

YOU CAN FEEL how cold it gets in your bones when fear blows its icy blast on your hopes. Or when death stalks cold and unfeeling outside the door of someone you love. Or when you can't escape the shivery dread of that dark storm cloud billowing on your horizon.

That's what John said: He said it was dark-cold in those hours after midnight. And after hours of broken sleep through Jesus' anguishing prayer in the writhing, shifting shadows of the Garden of Gethsemane, under the old, gnarled olive trees that stretched out their wizened limbs in prayer with Jesus, His disciples ached with the cold.

But for Jesus, there in the sacred ache of Gethsemane, the place that literally means "place of the olive press," the Lamb of God was being pressed with the crushing weight of every heinous and haunting darkness humanity has ever faced. His capillaries actually ruptured under the tightening vise of a whole cosmos of vice, and His pores couldn't stop leaking hot crimson passion down his brow. The disciples may have been chilled straight through, but the inferno of Jesus' heart burned with a white-hot passion that couldn't be doused for all eternity.

By the time they arrested Jesus and two of His disciples arrived at Annas's palace to be interrogated, an incident recorded only in the Gospel of John, Peter was desperate to warm his biting-cold fingertips, his chilled stiff neck over a fire kindled by the enemies of Christ. Try to warm your soul over the heat of any fire that isn't for the glory of the kingship of Christ, and you will scorch your only soul.

Though Peter would soon find himself taking heat in an interrogation in the outer courtyard, Jesus found Himself interrogated within.

Hands bound, Jesus was thrown in front of Annas. When they arrested Jesus, they only imagined they bound the God of the universe. The only thing that has ever bound Jesus is His love for you. The only thing in all the cosmos that has ever tied Christ's heart on this earth, to this earth, is the eternal cord of divine love to your very life. Because Jesus' heart is bound to you, your broken heart is bound together with hope.

You can trust all this to be true; you can trust that this isn't just some make-believe story, but actual, honest-to-God history, because Jesus was standing in the palace of Annas, the father-in-law of the high priest, Caiaphas. And Caiaphas's very name was discovered by construction workers who were widening a road just two miles south of Jerusalem, on a hill that today is known as "The Hill of Evil Counsel." Digging unintentionally into a Second Temple tomb, they unearthed an exceptionally ornate limestone bone box, inscribed in Aramaic with the words "Joseph son of Caiaphas," Joseph being the familiar name of the Jewish high priest now known as Caiaphas, who ruled in Jerusalem at the time of Jesus. Found with the stone bone box was a bronze coin minted in AD 43, during the reign of Herod Agrippa I. When the ancient lid of that small box, carved with a rare, intricate pattern of rosettes, with traces of red paint still noticeable along the edges, was lifted, there lay the cold, dry bones of the sixty-year-old Caiaphas, who, along with his father-in-law, Annas, effectively sent Jesus to His death. And found in the tomb with the stone box of the bones of Caiaphas? There were two Roman nails, consistent with crucifixion nails, with the end bent over to affix a hand to a cross. When studied under electron microscope analyses, the nails were shown to have ancient, microscopic fragments of bone and slivers of petrified wood accreted within the iron oxide rust.[1] Were these Roman nails found with Caiaphas used for crucifixion? Most likely. Whose crucifixion? Did Caiaphas, perhaps struggling with remorse over his family's role in the execution of the Son of God, keep two of the iron nails from the very passion of Christ and have them buried in the family tomb?

No one knows for certain if these were the nails of Jesus' crucifixion. But what is certain is that, even after two thousand years, there is clearly named, verifiable, historical, skeletal evidence of one key, prominent man named in the New Testament. What is certain is that the family of Annas and Caiaphas ended up as cold, dry bones in a darkened, chilled tomb, while the heart of the God-Man, whom they put on trial and crucified, burned with a love that defied death and still ignites hearts—across ages, across the globe, across pages, even in this moment.

The greatest love story is not just a story; this is actual *history.*

While Peter's heart may have turned cold toward Jesus while he was interrogated in the outer courtyard, Jesus' interrogation withstood flames from His own unwavering heat and passionate love: "Ask those who heard me," Jesus replied. "Surely they know what I said."

And your heart stirs, because your heart has heard Him, and you surely know who He really is. And if you know what He said—*all* of what He really said—how can your heart's affection not surely burn within, kindled to want His presence, His closeness, all of Him, most of all?

On trial, Christ did not need to defend Himself.

Because now we are *His* witnesses, even in the midst of our trials.

With each step of the pilgrimage, especially right now: How can your heart not burn within you?

PERSONAL NOTES TO SOUL FROM TODAY'S PILGRIMAGE INTO THE HEART OF JESUS:

BECAUSE

JESUS' HEART IS

BOUND TO YOU,

YOUR

BROKEN HEART

IS BOUND BACK

TOGETHER

WITH LOVE.

HOPE AFTER
A BROKEN WORD

"You aren't one of this man's disciples too, are you?"
she asked Peter.

He replied, "I am not."

. . . Meanwhile, Simon Peter was still standing
there warming himself. So they asked him, "You aren't
one of his disciples too, are you?"

He denied it, saying, "I am not."

One of the high priest's servants, a relative of the
man whose ear Peter had cut off, challenged him,
"Didn't I see you with him in the garden?" Again
Peter denied it, and at that moment a rooster began
to crow.

JOHN 18:17, 25-27

Day *34: At that moment a rooster began to crow. John 18:27*

YOU CAN STILL FEEL IT—what it's like to say something, do something that you thought you'd never say, swore you'd never do.

You know how you've been a Peter.

Peter moments are profoundly painful—when your bewildering words or actions betray your best intentions.

Jesus knows. This moment of Peter's life fulfills what He prophesied. Before this part of the story had ever been written, Jesus, the Word Himself, knew how these lines of the story would unfold. Back in the upper room, after the King of the universe had knelt low, taken the heels of His people, and washed away the filth between their toes, Simon Peter asked Jesus, "Lord, where are you going?"

Jesus replied, "Where I am going, you cannot follow now, but you will follow later."

Why could Peter not follow now? What, whether within or around, could possibly stop Peter from following Jesus now? Peter himself had asked, "Lord, why can't I follow you now? I will lay down my life for you."

It can be easy to think that we would lay down our lives for Christ when we struggle to daily stand up for Him and walk with Him.

Jesus answered, "Will you really lay down your life for me? Very truly I tell you, before the rooster crows, you will disown me three times!" (John 13:36-38).

Who dares to own that there are times when we, too, have disowned Him?

Everyone agrees that the hope—and the prayer—is simply this: People of the Word keep their word. People committed to Christ live out their commitments; people who depend on Christ are the most dependable; people in Christ are people of integrity.

Because you are made by the Word, it's the Word who gives you your identity, and your word is your identity. The word you keep is the person you ultimately become. You are your word. The word you keep to show up, to follow through, to deny self, is part of making you into who you are.

Not only does the Word give you your identity, but keeping your word gives you your community. Break your word, and you break community. Break your word to yourself, to your people enough times, and you break your identity.

Integrity, literally meaning "wholeness," is kin to the word *integer*, which is a whole number in mathematics; only a person of integrity is a whole person. A whole person isn't fragmented and fractioned into one person in private and another in public—otherwise you become a fraction of who you are made to be. Go back on your word, and you'll have to go back to find the parts of you that you've lost if you ever want to be whole again. Unless you keep your word, your promises, you keep losing yourself. Betray your promises to God, others, and yourself, and who have you become?

Yet . . . who of us can wholly keep our word? Who of us can keep all our promises and keep all of ourselves whole? Who hasn't been Peter and heard, in some soul-disappointing moment, some rooster crowing loudly, leaving us crying bitterly? Who hasn't tasted the stench and the sting, the burning smoke of another Peter-moment, when our lack of love lets us down, leaves us at the bottom of a pit. Yet at bottom, at base, underneath us still, is Love Himself.

Peter broke his word—but Jesus kept His Word to keep Peter. The Lamb of God went to the Cross to take every one of our Peter-moments, because He still takes us. Can you dare to believe His passionate love for you, even—especially—now? Can you dare to believe that even though Peter scorched his own soul with a string of denials because he felt the risk around Caiphas's fire too terrifying, the resurrected Love, who is Christ, gave Peter another chance? Can you hope to believe that after such a denial, Jesus would rise from the dead, light a fire on the beach, and invite Peter back into relationship with Him? And can you see it, how Peter would then turn, truly turn, though he was filled with the burning scent of great shame, but also with the heat of an even greater love? And in that moment, that Peter would hear Christ's humbling hospitality inviting him to come eat, to come and still be entrusted with work in the Kingdom, to feed Christ's sheep? Can you believe it for you?

Three times in front of all the people, Peter betrayed any love or commitment to Jesus—and then three times, Jesus committed what He loved most—His people—to this same Peter.

Do you love me? Feed my sheep.

Do you love me? Feed my sheep.
If you love me, feed my sheep.

Can you dare to believe there is still a gusher of love that cleans life's grime and any contamination on your conscience, and hushes the hauntings that howl in the hallways of your mind?

There was no way Peter could truly follow Jesus until Jesus first loved him enough to die for him. Only because Jesus followed the way of suffering to the Cross and took all our suffering can any of us now follow Him. The people who best keep their word to God are exactly the ones who know they can't. So they depend on *Him* to keep the whole covenant, to keep His Word, to be faithful, to keep them.

Nothing remakes everything like grace.

Your wreckage can still birth resurrection.

You can trust that what fixes all that's broken is to cast everything aside but His presence.

What feels like your destruction can yet be your reconstruction.

Nothing can ultimately ruin you—but only ruins you for anything less than God.

The most transformational life is a long repentance in His direction.

This is a pilgrimage worthy of your one life: What makes even us whiter than snow is melting into the depths of His unfathomable love.

PERSONAL NOTES TO SOUL FROM TODAY'S PILGRIMAGE INTO THE HEART OF JESUS:

NOTHING

REMAKES

EVERYTHING

LIKE GRACE.

THE KING OF YOUR HEART

So Pilate came out to them and asked, "What charges are you bringing against this man?"

"If he were not a criminal," they replied, "we would not have handed him over to you."

Pilate said, "Take him yourselves and judge him by your own law."

"But we have no right to execute anyone," they objected. This took place to fulfill what Jesus had said about the kind of death he was going to die.

Pilate then went back inside the palace, summoned Jesus and asked him, "Are you the king of the Jews?"

"Is that your own idea," Jesus asked, "or did others talk to you about me?"

"Am I a Jew?" Pilate replied. "Your own people and chief priests handed you over to me. What is it you have done?"

Jesus said, "My kingdom is not of this world. If it were, my servants would fight to prevent my arrest by the Jewish leaders. But now my kingdom is from another place."

"You are a king, then!" said Pilate.

Jesus answered, "You say that I am a king. In fact, the reason I was born and came into the world is to testify to the truth. Everyone on the side of truth listens to me."

Day 35: "My kingdom is not of this world." John 18:36

"What is truth?" retorted Pilate. With this he went out again to the Jews gathered there and said, "I find no basis for a charge against him. But it is your custom for me to release to you one prisoner at the time of the Passover. Do you want me to release 'the king of the Jews'?"

They shouted back, "No, not him! Give us Barabbas!" Now Barabbas had taken part in an uprising.

JOHN 18:29-40

YOUR HEART ANSWERS TO WHAT IT LOVES.

This is tender and true: Whatever you make much time for in your life ends up being the king of your life.

Ultimately, you crown what captivates you.

It's a tender and needful question: Is Love Himself your King, or have you overthrown Love Himself only to throw your heart at the feet of lesser, cheaper loves?

Jesus' eyes find yours: God only calls you to love Him with your whole heart because He knows anything you love more than Him will eventually break your heart in half.

Jesus' eyes hold yours: God only calls you to love Him with your whole heart so *you can be whole*.

Jesus gently cups your face close and whispers into the deepest part of your soul, "I have come that [you] may have life, and have it to the full" (John 10:10).

If you feel fragmented and fractured and less than full . . . what if now is the very moment that you're being given to trace the tender places in your heart to see whether you are loving the King of your heart with your whole heart?

Pilate asked Jesus point-blank: "Are you the king of the Jews?"

But Pilate didn't ask the bound Jesus about His kingship in front of the Jewish religious leaders. Because the Jewish leaders refused to step foot in Pilate's headquarters, lest they become ceremonially unclean. If

LOVED TO LIFE

they became unclean, they would have been unable to participate in the Passover celebrations. Ironically, the Jewish leaders wanted to be utmost careful to attend the Passover festivities, but they didn't attend to or show utmost care toward the actual Passover Lamb Himself. The Jewish leaders wanted to keep the Passover, while it was the true paschal Lamb Himself who hadn't kept or held anything back. He but let go of His throne and all of heaven to lay down His life for the sins of the world, out of love of the world, for the wholeness of the world and *fullness of real life*.

Why have fidelity more to the way your life looks or the way your life feels than genuine fidelity to Love Himself?

Why love keeping the letter of the law more than making your entire life into a love letter to the One who keeps you always?

Don't the questions beg your life for an answer?

The Sanhedrin, the council of Jewish leaders, had long since determined that Jesus had to be obliterated, erased from all conversation (John 11:47-53). Twice already they'd attempted to stone Jesus to death for blasphemy, for claiming to be God, for claiming to be the eternal King of the universe (John 8:59; 10:31).

There is no getting around it—in every line of the plotline of God, either Jesus is who He says He is—divine King—or He is a deluded conniver. There is no other way to categorize the otherworldly One who broke into time to liberate us into real life in Him and His Kingdom.

But the religious leaders, infuriated that Jesus would claim kingship not merely of an earthly realm but of a cosmic realm, now demanded that Jesus die a death of crucifixion, which was the exact fulfillment of Jesus' prophecy about His death: Just "as Moses lifted up the serpent in the wilderness, even so must the Son of Man be lifted up, that whoever believes in Him should not perish but have eternal life" (John 3:14-15, NKJV).

Jesus would not be buried under a pile of stones, a Light smothered under crushing darkness, but He would be lifted up, a Light on the heights to bring healing, to draw all those aching into the warmth of His comforting love and roll back all our stones of despair (John 12:32).

Jesus faced seven different hearings during his last twenty-four hours before being lifted up: first before Annas (John 18), then before Caiaphas

(Matthew 26), then before the Sanhedrin (Matthew 27), then on to Pilate (John 18), then before Herod (Luke 23), back to Pilate again (Luke 23), and finally before the people (John 18:38-40). Even in this trial before Pilate, there were seven scenes, moving from inside to outside Pilate's palace. But what if it's not Jesus who's actually the one on trial in the end?

What if it's the Pilate in each of us who's always really the one on trial? What if life is never so much about the trials we're facing but more about the posture of our own hearts in this midst of life-trials that's actually on trial?

What if Jesus stands before you now, heart bound to yours, eyes searching yours, heart whispering to yours, *Am I the King of your heart? Or what have you crowned with your time, your attention, your interest, your heart that can't raise you to real life in the end? Have you seen, really seen with the eyes of your heart, what I have done for you—so it moves you, moves you closer to My reviving heart? Has My love touched your heart, moved your heart, opened your heart, changed your heart, stirred your heart, stoked your heart, ignited your heart, inflamed your heart? Have you listened to all the ways I've been wooing you away from that which doesn't satisfy and back toward divine love and holy wholeness and the fullest life?*

Don't the questions beg your life for a real answer?

You can feel it in your bones right now, what He has done for you, for you, for *you*: He is the One who lived the perfect way you always hoped you would, and then offers the record of His life as your life. He's the One who died the painful way that could have been yours, and then He absorbed all your pain as His.

He's the One who heals broken hearts with His, the One who gives sight for every single one of your blind spots. He's the One who walks on the waves of your every storm, feeds you soul-manna in the midst of a multitude of troubles, crushes the head of every one of your hissing lies, raises your dead hopes back to life.

This is your everyday resurrection.

This is your everyday reality.

This is your everything.

Don't miss this.

He's pouring His life into your life. He is your Bread (John 6:35), your

Light (John 8:12), your Door (John 10:7), your Good Shepherd (John 10:11, 14), your Resurrection (John 11:25), your Way, your Truth, your Life (John 14:6), and your true Vine, the source of all your abundant life (John 15:1).

Don't miss Him.

He is your one King, your one Redeemer, your one Restorer, your one Sustainer, your one Lamb, Lover, and Lord—the only One whose passion has ever loved you to death and back to the safest, realest life because He saved us for *Himself,* who is the Life.

Pilgrimage into the palace of His presence and bow down.

Because Jesus really gets you—Jesus is the One who gets all of you. He gets you—so He gets all of you. The One who actually gets us, gets to have all our loyalties and our complete allegiance—our whole hearts, our whole lives, our whole selves—so we get to be whole. The King died to be the King of your heart . . . the King of your everything.

This changes everything—starting right now.

PERSONAL NOTES TO SOUL FROM TODAY'S PILGRIMAGE INTO THE HEART OF JESUS:

WHERE ARE
YOU FROM?

Then Pilate took Jesus and had him flogged. The soldiers twisted together a crown of thorns and put it on his head. They clothed him in a purple robe and went up to him again and again, saying, "Hail, king of the Jews!" And they slapped him in the face.

Once more Pilate came out and said to the Jews gathered there, "Look, I am bringing him out to you to let you know that I find no basis for a charge against him." When Jesus came out wearing the crown of thorns and the purple robe, Pilate said to them, "Here is the man!"

As soon as the chief priests and their officials saw him, they shouted, "Crucify! Crucify!"

But Pilate answered, "You take him and crucify him. As for me, I find no basis for a charge against him."

The Jewish leaders insisted, "We have a law, and according to that law he must die, because he claimed to be the Son of God."

When Pilate heard this, he was even more afraid, and he went back inside the palace. "Where do you come from?" he asked Jesus, but Jesus gave him no answer. "Do you refuse to speak to me?" Pilate said. "Don't you realize I have power either to free you or to crucify you?"

Day *36: "Where do you come from?" John 19:9*

Jesus answered, "You would have no power over me if it were not given to you from above. Therefore the one who handed me over to you is guilty of a greater sin."

From then on, Pilate tried to set Jesus free, but the Jewish leaders kept shouting, "If you let this man go, you are no friend of Caesar. Anyone who claims to be a king opposes Caesar."

When Pilate heard this, he brought Jesus out and sat down on the judge's seat at a place known as the Stone Pavement (which in Aramaic is Gabbatha). It was the day of Preparation of the Passover; it was about noon.

"Here is your king," Pilate said to the Jews.

But they shouted, "Take him away! Take him away! Crucify him!"

"Shall I crucify your king?" Pilate asked.

"We have no king but Caesar," the chief priests answered.

Finally Pilate handed him over to them to be crucified.

JOHN 19:1-16

LOOK INTO THE FACE of your Love, who came to die, to love you to the only life that fulfills.

He let the crown of thorns be pressed into His brow so you'd never be alone with that aching thorn pressed into your side.

He took the whips, made of leather strips with sharp metal and hooked bones, right down to the bloody bone to get you off every bloody hook. Your God was flogged to end your self-flagellation.

Your God, who breathed out whole starry galaxies, took the stinging slap to the cheek so you could turn your face toward a horizon of endless hope.

And your stricken Lamb didn't strike back, because He was lovestruck with you. Like a sheep before the shearers, He took it all so He could take all of you (Isaiah 53:7).

The Word-made-flesh let Himself become a pummeled, bloody mess to shield you against every word of accusation for all eternity.

Where else is there any real life apart from Love like this?

He came that you may have the full and realest life—but He doesn't force you to have this full life. He gives everyone a choice: Will we settle for fake or lesser versions of life—for cheap, unsatisfying knockoffs—or will we loosen ourselves from all the distractions and dupes, and embrace divine Love and Life Himself?

Pilate kept repeating himself: This Jesus had never done one thing wrong under the sun, not once in His entire life. Five times, Pilate fumbled attempts to release God from our arrest (Luke 23:4, 15, 20-22; John 19:4, 12-13). We may question Pilate's heart and ways—but in what ways are we, too, like Pilate and not fully arrested by God's love for us?

Maybe, Pilate wondered, if he had Jesus tortured sufficiently, would the people be sufficiently satisfied and free him? Strangely, Pilate mused that if he humiliated God enough, that might be enough to liberate God. Spit on and bloodied with beatings, wouldn't God now just be spewed out onto the streets by the people? Wouldn't they finally pity the battered and bruised Lamb of God and just let Him go free? How could this mockery of some deranged King be of any danger to the power of the elite?

But the crowd and those in power wanted Him dead—not merely because He claimed to sit on the throne as King of the Jews, but ultimately because they knew He actually claimed to be God on the throne, as King of the universe.

Hadn't otherworldly words already passed Jesus' lips that He was King of a Kingdom not of this world (John 18:36)? Either Jesus is unhinged—or the whole of the universe hinges on Him. Either banish Him or bow before Him as King—just don't belittle Him into being some tame teacher of your own making.

Pilate could sense that Jesus wasn't deranged, and He wasn't a demagogue—Jesus was divine. Which is to say, earth is a called-on planet. This isn't an accidental planet, this isn't a coincidental planet, this isn't a random planet—this is a called-on planet.

The passionate love of God moved God to actually come and walk the sod of this planet because He wanted to walk next to you, to be with you, to call on you, because He has a singular call for you. This is the truest story: The Divine wants to dwell with you, to live in you.

And perhaps that's why Pilate stood looking into the eyes of the Christ and was "even more afraid." When very God wants to dwell within you, you may experience some awed fear within.

Pilate's attempts to manipulate the release of Jesus weren't out of anger or out of amusement; Pilate was actually acting out of awe. Because Roman belief at the time held that the gods on high could come down in human guise. Pilate knew that as he looked into the face of the Man before him, he was looking into the face of more than a man—he was looking into the face of the Maker of man; he was looking into the face of the Source of the universe; he was looking into the face of infinite Love. How could you not be awed by God? How could you not stammer out, "Where do you come from?"

There is perhaps no more important question in the universe than to look into the face of Jesus and ask, "Where are You from?" Because we first have to know where Jesus is from before we can determine, "Where do we go from here?" Once you know where Jesus is from, you can determine where you're going with your whole life. If you know that Jesus is ultimately from on high, what else can you possibly do but bend down low and surrender your whole heart to Him? If you know that Jesus is God who came down from heaven to actually walk this earth, you know the way to walk out all your days on earth till you walk right back into your home of heaven.

Know that Jesus came to you from the throne room of heaven, and you know that He alone is worthy to sit on the throne of your heart. *And you dethrone any and all distractions.*

"Don't you realize I have power?" Pilate was in awe that Jesus wasn't afraid of his power. Jesus wasn't afraid, because He knew that condemnation doesn't hold power, diagnoses don't hold power, shame doesn't hold power, the past doesn't hold power—*God alone holds power over everything that seems to have power.* God is for you and holds you and uses all the power of His love to save you into the heart of Him who is Life.

Offering the beaten, sacrificial Lamb of God back to the people, Pilate

LOVED TO LIFE

was stunned that the crowd wasn't moved in the least to release Him but kept crying, "Crucify him!"

How many times have our days, our decisions with our time, our distractions to numb ourselves with quick dopamine hits all said in their own way, "Away with Jesus, away with Jesus" instead of committing to Jesus and recognizing that withness with Him is the only way to the wholeness we seek?

How many times are we like Pilate, lacking the courage of conviction? How many times are we like Pilate, failing to have the character of commitment, betraying the conscience within to gain the acceptance of the crowd? How many times have we rejected Jesus as the King of our loves, only to find ourselves enslaved by cheaper tyrant-loves?

Because every single moment, every heart keeps choosing who is its king. Every heart comes with a throne that is seeking every moment to be filled. And either Jesus is the King of your heart, the only One who has ever loved you to death and back to the fullest, realest life in the Kingdom of Himself, or a million oppressive Caesars will rule your heart to death.

Yet everything changes when you take the time to fully linger here: When you bear witness to His passion for you, how can you not bear any cross for Him?

When you touch His wounds and touch the edges of the depth of His love for you, your heart becomes bound to His. When you slow-trace His every scar and see how you're tracing your own name, you can't stop saying His name.

Look Him long in the eye—straight through to His heart rent wide open for you.

Here is your pilgrimage into the presence of pure Love that fully transforms your heart, if you will let yourself be fully receptive to Him.

Here is the greatest passion you have ever known.

Here is your everything . . . your real life.

PERSONAL NOTES TO SOUL FROM TODAY'S PILGRIMAGE INTO THE HEART OF JESUS:

JESUS ALONE

IS WORTHY

TO SIT ON

THE THRONE

OF YOUR

HEART.

THE REVOLUTIONARY CENTER

So they took Jesus, and he went out, bearing his own cross, to the place called The Place of a Skull, which in Aramaic is called Golgotha. There they crucified him, and with him two others, one on either side, and Jesus between them. Pilate also wrote an inscription and put it on the cross. It read, "Jesus of Nazareth, the King of the Jews." Many of the Jews read this inscription, for the place where Jesus was crucified was near the city, and it was written in Aramaic, in Latin, and in Greek. So the chief priests of the Jews said to Pilate, "Do not write, 'The King of the Jews,' but rather, 'This man said, I am King of the Jews.'" Pilate answered, "What I have written I have written."

When the soldiers had crucified Jesus, they took his garments and divided them into four parts, one part for each soldier; also his tunic. But the tunic was seamless, woven in one piece from top to bottom, so they said to one another, "Let us not tear it, but cast lots for it to see whose it shall be." This was to fulfill the Scripture which says,

"They divided my garments among them, and for my clothing they cast lots."

So the soldiers did these things, but standing by the cross of Jesus were his mother and his mother's sister, Mary the wife of Clopas, and

Day *37: There they crucified him. John 19:18*

Mary Magdalene. When Jesus saw his mother and the disciple whom he loved standing nearby, he said to his mother, "Woman, behold, your son!" Then he said to the disciple, "Behold, your mother!" And from that hour the disciple took her to his own home.

JOHN 19:16-27, ESV

THIS IS THE HOUR He pours out His passion for you and the revolution of His love turns everything around for you.

Jesus hangs naked on a tree at Calvary, only to cover all the shame of humanity since Adam and Eve hid ashamed behind that first Garden of Eden tree.

Jesus is exiled and crucified, only to return all of humanity back to the paradise of communion with God that Adam and Eve's sin had exiled us all from.

Jesus drinks the cup of suffering to do the will of His Father, only to revive all of humanity who have been suffering since Adam and Eve ate of that first tree directly against the will of their Father.

Jesus takes a crown of thorns, only to offer real rescue to all of humanity who, since Adam and Eve's rejection of God, have been under a curse of thorns.

Jesus gives up His life on a tree, only to "give the right to eat from the tree of life, which is in the paradise of God" (Revelation 2:7). Jesus gives up His life, only to revolutionize our lives toward the abundant life we've craved since Adam and Eve disobeyed and ate from the tree of life and began to die (Genesis 3:24).

Love Himself giving up His life for you on that Cross—this is what reverses all death's power over you. And the power of Love turns everything toward life for you, and life to the full.

Jesus bears His cross for you, but it is you He is carrying.

Slung across his wounded shoulders, that cross beam weighed more than one hundred pounds. But it was the brokenness and sinfulness of the world, your world, that crushed Him immeasurably, that drove the King of the universe into a love revolution to win you back to life and to Himself.

This is what Pilate had inscribed on a placard on the cross: "Jesus of Nazareth, the King of the Jews." It was customary to create such a sign for the condemned person, stating his name and the nature of his crime. But in Jesus' case, the charge wasn't that He claimed to be the King but that *He actually was*. Written in three languages (Aramaic, Latin, and Greek), the sign heralded this moment in history as an international, global, cosmic event. It announced that Jesus was not just King to one people, but King of the world—the cosmic King whose very Kingdom is not of this world, but an otherworldly realm of love where real life flourishes.

God-with-skin-on came to this sod; God-with-skin-on visited this planet. God-with-skin-on is more than theology—God-with-skin-on stepped into literal geography because He wanted nothing less than to experience personal intimacy with you.

When He laid His own shredded back down on the wood, He did it not because He was forced to; the Lamb of God willingly laid down His life for His friends, for you, to cover your brokenness and sinfulness with His perfection, to cover you with a robe of rightness and make you His bride. The One who is Love was slain by love, for love. He was love-slain for you so you could rise to the realest life in the inner chambers of His heart.

With arms flung along that cross-beam, the supernatural hands that flung stars across the canvas of whole galaxies were slammed with spikes formed from metallic elements He Himself created in the core of the very planet that He came to visit.

And then God-in-the-flesh let seven-inch spikes pierce the heels of His feet, the only feet to have ever walked across surging waves, the feet of the One who is the only way, the truest truth, the realest life.

"They crucified him."

Three unadorned words. Like another three words, as if this were Christ's cosmic heart-cry across all of time and space: *I love you.*

The apostle John's Gospel need not explain or embellish the horrors of crucifixion; it simply states the most arresting story. The created crucified their Creator.

Cicero, the Roman noble, spoke of crucifixion as an unspeakable punishment, worse than beheading or burning: "What shall I say of crucifying [someone]? . . . An action cannot by any possibility be adequately expressed by any name bad enough for it."[1]

There are no words when you slay the Word.

Humanity crucifies God.

Because it broke His heart to see how we flit to all kinds of flimsy loves, all our love affairs with the betraying things of this world, He lay down His bare, bruised, and beating heart on that cross-altar of wood to woo and win us back to Himself and to the only Love that can breathe life into all our fractured hearts.

God surrendered Himself to death by crucifixion to cover our sins and restore us to communion with Him, which is the definition of real life.

And it's there at Calvary that the whole of the world is represented, with Jesus at the center, and on one side, the needy repentant who was saved, and on the other, the self-reliant who was unsaved. In the center was the revolutionary linchpin of everything, the passionate King, the center of the universe. He alone was centered in history, centered between hope and all kinds of hell, centered between God and all of humanity, centered between restoration and all kinds of condemnation, centered between abandonment and at-one-ment.

For six agonizing hours, the God who hung the sun, hung in the sun. But love drove Him to turn everything around, drove Him to the very nth degree—even to death—so that nothing would pluck us from His hand.

Don't brush past this.

He'd been the one to bend low to kiss warm breath into the lungs of humanity, and now, physically fastened to a wooden pole, His every heaving breath was a fireball of agony ripping through His lungs until He who gave breath could barely bear to heave one more searing breath.

Your Lamb bled out . . . for you, for you, *for you.*

God has always sacrificed for you. Love has always sacrificed for you.

In Hebrew, the word for sacrifice, *korban*, means "to draw nearer." Love Himself has always sacrificed Himself for you, to make a way to be nearer to you, to be intimately one with you, to take care of you.

This is what makes this singular day in history not only good but unequivocally the *best*: You get to never be abandoned because He abandoned *everything* to be with *you*.

You get kinship with God because of His crucified kingship, because He shed His blood to make you His very blood, to make you His very own. You get to call the King of the universe your very own Father and live forever in a new kind of family of cruciform love, because the Son of God loved you to death, to put to death every one of the old ways that malformed your heart, your life.

This is relief. This is revolutionary. *This is all about relationship.*

His atonement on the Cross was for nothing less than at-one-ment with you. Because He knows and wants this for you: At-one-ment with God is the only way for a soul to be wholly at peace. Good Friday is truly Best Friday, because what could best this?

How could anyone keep a revolutionary love like this to themselves when He gave all of Himself to rescue us from all of ourselves? How could anyone be ashamed to share a revolutionary love like this when He took every last ounce of our shame? How could anyone hesitate to hold back the revolutionary Good News on Good Friday when He let go of everything to hold us for forever?

He took fire so you could walk free. He took violence so you could be a victor. He took hell so you could be healed and begin to savor a taste of heaven now. Your sin hurt Him far more sharply than any spike could, and He let the horrors of Satan take a swipe at Him so that every single one of our heartbreaking sins could be wiped clean.

What Jesus gave you on the Cross was a love so indescribable that all other words fail to express what painful depths He went through for you—a revolutionary love that was so literally beyond words that a completely new word had to be forged to define this otherworldly love: *excruciating*. From two Latin words, *ex cruciatus* ("excruciating") literally means "out of the cross."

Out of the cross, excruciating love turns the darkness around to light.

Out of the cross, excruciating love turns all brokenness around to wholeness.

Out of the cross, excruciating love turns the walking dead around toward glorious life.

Out of the cross, excruciating love turns to *you*.

Out of the cross, excruciating Love Himself ushers you into communion with Him, *and this is the fullest life*.

Out of the cross, this excruciating love that's completely revolutionary, that turns the whole of the universe around—it begins this great revolution within your own heart toward Life and Love Himself.

PERSONAL NOTES TO SOUL FROM TODAY'S PILGRIMAGE INTO THE HEART OF JESUS:

OUT OF

THE CROSS,

EXCRUCIATING LOVE

TURNS THE

WALKING DEAD

AROUND TOWARD

GLORIOUS LIFE.

PIERCED

After this, Jesus, knowing that all was now finished, said (to fulfill the Scripture), "I thirst." A jar full of sour wine stood there, so they put a sponge full of the sour wine on a hyssop branch and held it to his mouth. When Jesus had received the sour wine, he said, "It is finished," and he bowed his head and gave up his spirit.

Since it was the day of Preparation, and so that the bodies would not remain on the cross on the Sabbath (for that Sabbath was a high day), the Jews asked Pilate that their legs might be broken and that they might be taken away.

So the soldiers came and broke the legs of the first, and of the other who had been crucified with him. But when they came to Jesus and saw that he was already dead, they did not break his legs. But one of the soldiers pierced his side with a spear, and at once there came out blood and water. He who saw it has borne witness—his testimony is true, and he knows that he is telling the truth—that you also may believe. For these things took place that the Scripture might be fulfilled: "Not one of his bones will be broken." And again another Scripture says, "They will look on him whom they have pierced."

JOHN 19:28-37, ESV

Day *38: "They will look on him whom they have pierced." John 19:37*

God, who is the breath of life, who breathed warm life into the lungs of the very first man, now death-gurgles to breathe.

The full weight of His body, stripped and suspended to the cross, painfully stresses the diaphragm of the Divine.

The only way for Him to exhale is to thrust up more than twelve inches from His pierced feet, nails slamming against tarsal bones, His raw back scraping up the rough bark of the cross with every desperate breath. Crucifixion is often this slow death by asphyxiation. This is breathtaking love.

For all the times you felt like you were suffocating under all the overwhelm, Jesus now, with every gasp for air, suffocates with overwhelming love for you, to overcome whatever you're up against.

Carbon dioxide rises in His blood. Muscles violently cramp. His heart pounds wild, pumping every iota of available oxygen to weakening tissue. Capillaries leak. His breathing shallows, speeds, turns to frantic gasping. He's hungry for air. He's hungry enough for you to grasp your attention, your whole heart—to do this for you.

His arms, excruciatingly extended across the span of the beam, scream with the weight of His body that stretches them more than six inches longer than normal. He will go to any lengths to be with you.

Water builds around His heart, crushing His lungs. It's been more than fifteen hours since any water has passed His parched and bloody lips. Scourged and flogged, severely dehydrated, with high potassium levels surging in His bloodstream, the heart of God is sent dangerously galloping. God never stops coming for you, running for you.

Enduring incomprehensible burn with every thrusting breath, Jesus, the Word, forces air to pass over vocal cords, because, regardless of the agony, the Word needs to speak not once but seven times on the Cross— words that cannot go unspoken, words that you have to know He said, to set all the records straight: "Forgive them" (Luke 23:34).

He forgave you, to get you . . . to get all of you.

"You will be with me in paradise" (Luke 23:43). Jesus endured hell because He saw how you—*you*— could be with Him in paradise.

God, who hung every star, hangs by two iron spikes, nails through wrists, and He isn't hanging on for dear life but is giving up His life because He wants to hold on to you, to give you real life in the paradise that is His presence.

He looks you in the eye. Your heart hears His parched whisper: "I thirst."

Your dying God thirsts because He's parched to completely drink down the cup of wrath that was rightly meant for you because of all the falling short from always acting rightly. Your God endures the worst for you so that when your soul thirsts, you can drink deeply of the only love that actually satisfies your craving soul. How can you not deeply thirst for more of Him?

Just like the hyssop was once saturated with the blood of the lamb to mark the doorposts of your ancestors in Egypt so the angel of death might pass over them, so the hyssop now saturates the sour wine and is held up to the parched and cracked lips of your Passover Lamb so death and despair and destruction might forever pass over you.

The bitter vinegar on hyssop wets His lips. His body contorts, all these searing currents of pain spasming cramped muscles. His shoulders, wrists, elbows increasingly dislocate with His aching body weight. The prophecy of the psalmist in Psalm 22 is fulfilled, and there's the breaking heart of the hanging, crucified God:

I am poured out like water,
and all my bones are out of joint.
My heart has turned to wax;
it has melted within me.
My mouth is dried up like a potsherd,
and my tongue sticks to the roof of my mouth;
you lay me in the dust of death.

Dogs surround me,
a pack of villains encircles me;
they pierce my hands and my feet.
All my bones are on display;
people stare and gloat over me.

They divide my clothes among them
and cast lots for my garment.

PSALM 22:14-18

Your God flails, exposed and naked, to cover every time you've failed, every time you've been shamefully exposed.

"God made him who had no sin to be sin for us, so that in him we might become the righteousness of God" (2 Corinthians 5:21). This is the gospel. "Come and see the victories of the cross. . . . Christ's wounds are thy healing, his agonies thy repose, his conflicts thy conquests, his groans thy songs, his pains thine ease, his shame thy glory, his death thy life, his suffering thy salvation."[1]

His blood pressure drops. With every upward thrust and gasp for breath, the two crushed median nerves in His wrists detonate lava pain through His veins, and Jesus howls with all of humanity, His cry reverberating off the walls of every hurting heart: "My God, my God, why have you forsaken me?" (Matthew 27:46).

Jesus doesn't save Himself so He can save you.

Jesus is forsaken in every way so you will never be forsaken by the only One who is the Way, the Truth, the Life.

With His arms fully extended on that cross, Jesus, who is no less than fully God, proves that God is passionate about you. The passion of Christ for you on the Cross proves that God has *always* been passionate about you. "We must not . . . speak of God punishing Jesus, or of Jesus persuading God, for to do so is to set them over against each other as if they acted independently of each other or were even in conflict with each other," writes the esteemed theologian John Stott. "Whatever happened on the cross in terms of 'God-forsakenness' was voluntarily accepted by both in the same holy love. . . . Divine love triumphed over divine wrath by divine self-sacrifice."[2]

Look long at His side, His face, His arms, stretched open wide for you, and feel the reality of what happens at the Cross.

The atonement that happens at the Cross happens because God gave

God to satisfy God—to satisfy your every longing in the only Love who has loved you to death and back to the fullest life, because He Himself is Life.

The passionate love of God isn't satisfied until God is at-one with you.

Struggling up through scalding pain for the next breath, the combined forces of His love, hypoxia (too little oxygen), and hypercapnia (too much carbon dioxide), His heart beats into this furious tachycardia, his pulse pounding at more than two hundred beats per minute. His lungs succumb to pulmonary edema. Plasma and blood press like a vice around His wild heart. The heart of God beats out of control, with an uncontrollable love for you.

And now the whole of the universe reverberates with His love cry: *Tetelestai.* "It is finished!" It is complete! This is not the wail of the wounded; this is the Lover's loud cry of victory.

Your every sin is covered.

Your soul's enemy, evil itself, is finished, defeated.

God's love for you is wholly complete.

There is nothing you can do, nothing you need to do, nothing you ever can do to complete this love further. Everything is now accomplished, finished, done, complete. All prophecy about the coming Messiah is complete, all power of sin is finished, all that is needed is now accomplished. Jesus said it on the cross: "It is complete," because you are completely loved.

His cry of completion on the cross is the cry of a fulfilled love, so you can experience a fulfilled life. Because your every shortcoming has been paid in full, you are finally fulfilled.

And now, His artery walls, weakened from the flogging, from falling hard under the weight of the cross, from the inhumane torture and trauma, compress the heart of God between sternum and spinal column. Now, the decreased oxygen in His lungs mercilessly shrivels the tissues of His heart. Now, Christ's heart catastrophically thunders.

And now, in the erupting pain of the last few seconds, the Word speaks one more time, because Jesus' last words are not "It is finished." The Word still has seven last words pressing on His slamming heart. With His very last surge of earthly strength, He drives the heels of His pierced and shattered feet against the iron nails, strikes a crushing blow to the head of Satan, and then the conquering God uses His final burning breath to gift us these words to live the whole of life by: "Into your hands I commit my spirit."

His pulse explodes. Arteries climactically seize. The heart of Jesus ruptures.

The immeasurable heart of God bursts with infinite love.

And the prophecy is literally fulfilled: "Reproach and insults have broken my heart" (Psalm 69:20, AMP).

Christ dies of a broken heart so you can fully live with a whole one.

Jesus sacrifices His own broken and contrite heart to *heal your broken and craving heart.*

Jesus takes the crushing ache and heartbreak and sins of the entire world into His own heart (John 1:29) and, absorbing every last iota of it all, His heart ultimately explodes with love—with love *for you.*

The head of Christ falls. "Christ, our paschal lamb, has been sacrificed" (1 Corinthians 5:7, RSV). Normally, the bones of those crucified are smashed and broken, so the one on the cross is violently incapacitated from being able to push-struggle up to gasp for air, so they death-gurgle and suffocate faster. But exactly like the perfect Passover lamb in Egypt was decreed to not have one bone of its body broken (Numbers 9:12), so your own sacrificial Lamb, Jesus, has not one broken bone in His body—*to perfectly heal your soul.*

Bowed and surrendered, Jesus gives His spirit to God.

With His very last breath before death, Jesus whispers that the best place for all of life is in the hands of God.

Everything is finished only when everything is entrusted into God's hands.

The hands that went to Calvary, the hands that took the nails and a cosmos of pain to rescue you, are the safest hands in the world to entrust your whole world to.

Into Your pierced hands, Lord, we entrust this begging hope.

Into Your nailed hands, Lord, we commit this bruised and tender relationship.

Into Your healing hands, Lord, we entrust this impossible situation, this dream, this child, this heartbreak, this no-way-out.

It's only life lived in the love of His scarred hands that can ever heal you. Only the scarred hands of God can keep you forever soul-safe.

Now, after His very last words on that cross, after He has breathed His last, after everything is finished and complete and given to God, the razor-sharp edge of a spear slices open the soft skin of Christ, and "at once there came out blood and water."

This happened.

In the pleural, hollow cavity between lung and rib cage, Christ's blood pooled and separated, the heavier red cells settling, the watery plasma rising. This moment had an actual witness who testified that he saw with his own eyes how blood and water poured, hemorrhaged, out the side of the crucified God. This had to happen, because, "without the shedding of blood there is no forgiveness of sins" (Hebrews 9:22). This happened because there isn't one of us whose life doesn't need to be redeemed—signified by the blood and then reborn to real life—signified by the water. This is the moment that not only satisfies God but satisfies every craving thirst you've ever known.

Jesus "poured out his life unto death" (Isaiah 53:12) so that you could be filled with the full life experienced only in Life Himself. The word for soul in Hebrew, *nephesh*, is the same word that is often translated "life." Jesus pours out His soul for you, and the blood and the water flow from His side, and He releases His life *to release you to life.*

Here, His death-water is your very life-water.

Here, your deepest wounds and staining sins are cleansed by this water.

Here, today, in this very moment, you are fulfilling the prophecy of Zechariah, and you can feel the sacred, ancient words stirring within you: "I will pour out a spirit of compassion . . . so that, when they look on the one whom they have pierced, they shall mourn for him . . . and weep bitterly over him" (Zechariah 12:10, NRSV).

Here at the Cross, your heart is completely broken—and completely healed.

Here at the Cross, you see what you have done to Him—*and what He has done for you.*

Here your heart is rent wide open: "By the cross, I know the gravity of my sin toward God, and the greatness of God's love toward me."[3]

Here at the Cross, the horrible heartbreak *done by us* is made, through the perfect heart of the crucified One, into heart healing *done for us*.

As the poet John Donne wrote, "All his life was a continual passion." *For you.*[4]

All of history and prophecy—and every other word of Scripture—is fulfilled: "Christ loved us and gave himself up for us" (Ephesians 5:2, esv).

This is where you find your God—not weighing your life with a set of scales, but here on a cross with His arms stretched wide to embrace and save all of you.

It's only a personal encounter with the Cross and the person of Christ that can wholly transform the heart of the person you are.

Your life pilgrimage has led to this moment.

Look on Him.

Behold the Lamb of God, who takes away the sins of the world (John 1:29).

Behold the only Love who takes all of you, the only One who loves you to death and gives you His whole, perfect life.

PERSONAL NOTES TO SOUL FROM TODAY'S PILGRIMAGE INTO THE HEART OF JESUS:

JESUS DOESN'T

SAVE HIMSELF–

SO HE CAN

SAVE YOU . . .

FOR HIMSELF.

SALVATION SATURDAY

Later, Joseph of Arimathea asked Pilate for the body of Jesus. Now Joseph was a disciple of Jesus, but secretly because he feared the Jewish leaders. With Pilate's permission, he came and took the body away. He was accompanied by Nicodemus, the man who earlier had visited Jesus at night. Nicodemus brought a mixture of myrrh and aloes, about seventy-five pounds. Taking Jesus' body, the two of them wrapped it, with the spices, in strips of linen. This was in accordance with Jewish burial customs. At the place where Jesus was crucified, there was a garden, and in the garden a new tomb, in which no one had ever been laid. Because it was the Jewish day of Preparation and since the tomb was nearby, they laid Jesus there.

JOHN 19:38-42

Day 39: *They laid Jesus there. John 19:42*

YOU'VE KNOWN DAYS of smashed and dashed hopes.

You know what it feels like to be staggering, stumbling through "What now?" days.

You've been so gutted and stung by how the story has gone you just feel numb.

And the tomb is pitch-thick dark.

The silence is deep. Motionless.

Under the shroud, God is lifeless—clammy and cold.

The stomachs of the disciples churn and knot, nauseous.

The One who said He is the Way, the Truth, the Life—is dead.

And they've hung every last ounce of their hope on the Man who hung on a cross—who is now a rotting corpse in a damp grave.

The tomb has devoured all their hope. Their hearts are bereft, broken, empty—and full of bewildering, confusing grief.

Where is God now? Where are all His promises now? Where is the goodness of God now?

Who doesn't have the grief of a tomb of buried hope somewhere in their story?

You have to believe that when it looks like God is dead to you, God is still at work all around you.

You may feel the ache of living in the long, dark Saturday between Good Friday and Resurrection Sunday; you may deeply feel like you live in the excruciating wait of Saturday. And yet, still, the reality is this:

Wherever you are silently waiting, God is seriously working.

When you feel the nothingness of God, nothing could be further from the truth.

Where you sense silence, God's presence is silently reworking all the world.

This isn't quietly reposing Saturday; this is *Rescue Saturday*.

This isn't hushed, silent Saturday; this is *Salvation Saturday*.

This isn't slumbering, drowsing Saturday; this is *Deliverance Saturday*.

You can let everything become still now.

You can let all your aching questions and doubts and disappointments sit next to the possibilities of holy miracles.

Something sacred and otherworldly is stirring.

You can trust: Every new life has always been born out of the very darkest place.

Exactly when you think Jesus is painfully inactive is when He is purposefully inundating the gates of hell for you.

When Jesus turns to the thief on the cross and says, "Today you will be with me in paradise" (Luke 23:43), you catch a glimpse of what Jesus is doing between His death and resurrection *for you*. How the triune God is both welcoming the thief into paradise that very day and storming the gates of Hades on behalf of that thief—and *for you*.

In those long hours on Saturday, between Good Friday and Resurrection Sunday, Jesus doesn't go the way of all humanity; Jesus is the singular human who goes to the gates of Hades to destroy evil and become the very way out of the darkness for all of humanity.

Those doors of death that opened and devoured every other soul who ever lived are now open by the One who is Himself the Door, the One who lays down His life for you. He lays those doors of death flat, because the Lamb of God will stop at nothing to enfold every lamb from His fold—*you*—in His arms for all eternity. "For you know that it was not with perishable things such as silver or gold that you were redeemed from the empty way of life handed down to you from your ancestors, but with the precious blood of Christ, a lamb without blemish or defect" (1 Peter 1:18-19).

The One who stretched out His arms on that cross with your name etched into the palms of His hands is the One who, on Salvation Saturday, disarmed Death itself and tore open the gates of Hades to enfold all the dead who loved Him, all who died under the Old Testament covenant, before Christ's sacrifice on the Cross. Though the body of Jesus lay in the tomb, the love of Jesus gathered all those resting in Hades and Abraham's bosom to Himself (Luke 16:22).

"Silent Saturday" is anything but silent because His Word speaks of how Jesus descended and preached to the souls in Hades: "He went and proclaimed God's salvation to earlier generations who ended up in the prison of judgment because they wouldn't listen" (1 Peter 3:19, MSG). As the good shepherd goes in search of his lost sheep, the crucified and buried Jesus descended into the depths, the entombed One going to the ends of the world for the love of the bound, to take the hands of the dead in Hades and all the walking dead here and whisper, "Awake, O sleeper, and arise from the dead, and Christ will shine on you" (Ephesians 5:14, ESV).

Jesus broke the seeming silence of Saturday, and in the stillness of your soul, as you linger and gaze on Him, can you hear the truth of His love for you?

For the love of you, your first Love descended below, to bust all who love Him out of the pit. Because you were made not to be in any hellish bondage but to be bonded to Him.

Your first Love went beneath the earth, beneath your every shame and failure and unspoken broken to lift you above your nightmare, to raise you above everything that drags you down, to raise you up to the heights of heaven so you could share divine communion with Him endlessly.

Your first Love became the One no one helped, to forever become your sure help, to become the help of the helpless, to be where all your true help comes from. So come to Him.

Your first Love wept excruciating drops of blood in a garden, then was shamefully crucified and buried in a garden tomb to win back you who once listened to lies and turned from His love in the first Garden. Your first Love nailed down His eternal love for you on Calvary's Tree to give you infinitely more than anything you've ever reached for from Eden's tree.

And right now, your first Love is restoring your soul to more than any earthly paradise; He is restoring you to the *greater paradise of His heart*. And there's not an eye or ear or mind anywhere that could even dare to imagine what fulfilling joy He is preparing for you who love Him and simply want Him for all eternity.

There is nothing silent about today.

Who dares to presume exactly what it means when Jesus said, "Just as Jonah was three days and three nights in the belly of the great fish, so will the Son of Man be three days and three nights in the heart of the earth" (Matthew 12:40, ESV)? But you have to know, beyond any shadow of a doubt, that He did it to woo and win your heart to His and that there was nothing silent about it. Because just as Jonah sang in the belly of the fish with "shouts of grateful praise" (Jonah 2:9), so Jesus descended with a love song on His lips to the triune God, who rocked the very foundations of hell for love of you.

All of Salvation Saturday, which is anything but silent, speaks to you: You don't have anything to fear in the dark or the stillness or the waiting or the questions or even in the most disorienting grief. Terrible things can happen in this world—and yet God does miraculous things in tombs.

Henri Nouwen said, "If the God who revealed life to us, and whose only desire is to bring us to life, loved us so much that he wanted to experience with us the total absurdity of death, then—yes, then there must be hope; then there must be something more than death; then there must be a promise that is not fulfilled in our short existence in this world."[1]

On the days when it all feels too much—that's exactly when God is doing much more than you could ever imagine.

The days when God feels silent are exactly the days when God is silently slaying evil to ultimately win your freedom into the fullest life.

PERSONAL NOTES TO SOUL FROM TODAY'S PILGRIMAGE INTO THE HEART OF JESUS:

THE MOMENT EVERYTHING CHANGES

Early on the first day of the week, while it was still dark, Mary Magdalene went to the tomb and saw that the stone had been removed from the entrance. So she came running to Simon Peter and the other disciple, the one Jesus loved, and said, "They have taken the Lord out of the tomb, and we don't know where they have put him!" . . .

Now Mary stood outside the tomb crying. As she wept, she bent over to look into the tomb and saw two angels in white, seated where Jesus' body had been, one at the head and the other at the foot.

They asked her, "Woman, why are you crying?"

"They have taken my Lord away," she said, "and I don't know where they have put him." At this, she turned around and saw Jesus standing there, but she did not realize that it was Jesus.

He asked her, "Woman, why are you crying? Who is it you are looking for?"

Thinking he was the gardener, she said, "Sir, if you have carried him away, tell me where you have put him, and I will get him."

Jesus said to her, "Mary."

She turned toward him and cried out in Aramaic, "Rabboni!" (which means "Teacher").

Day 40: "I have seen the Lord!" John 20:18

Jesus said, "Do not hold on to me, for I have not yet ascended to the Father. Go instead to my brothers and tell them, 'I am ascending to my Father and your Father, to my God and your God.'"

Mary Magdalene went to the disciples with the news: "I have seen the Lord!" And she told them that he had said these things to her.

JOHN 20:1-2, 11-18

HERE AND NOW: Your past story closes shut with the Cross, and your whole new story opens up with the rolled-away stone and the Resurrection.

Now is your new beginning.

This is the remaking of you and the whole world. The movement of that stone on Resurrection Sunday started a resurrection movement that's now moving through you and the entire universe.

There is nothing greater than this. First one rotting cell sparks in the tomb, then a heart valve quivers in the pitch-dark. The dead God has a pulse. The universe quakes with hope.

While a beetle scratches in the dark of the tomb, the cornerstone of Christianity is rising, and the concave chest cavity of God shudders in the cold. Sunken death is inflated with His hot breath, and atoms of the second Adam are recreated, resurrected, beginning to turn around the whole of the cosmos. In the shadows of that clammy tomb, the chamber of the heart of God begins to pound in His chest like He's pounding at the door of your own tomb.

Because He knew that only if you let in an undying love like His can you ever know the way out to life.

His scar-mangled hands take the slow, careful moments to fold His grave clothes, like He is tenderly dressing your own wounds, wrapping your rawest places so new hope can always unfold in you.

It happened—this all happened.

Because blood began to pump a revolution of hope through the veins of God, because that stone made one revolution in front of the tomb of

God, the revolution of the entire universe begins, and it turns everything around for you. The Love that moved straight through death and right out of the tomb now moves you into a whole new way of being in the world.

The Resurrection is more than some supernatural spectacle, more than a harbinger of heaven; the Resurrection is the revolution of the cosmos, the Kingdom of God, and your whole life.

This is not metaphor. This is miracle made material.

The Word-made-flesh was bodily resurrected in the flesh. This is *anastasis*—this is resurrection, the bodily dead becoming bodily alive. This is the linchpin of Christianity, the crux of Christianity, the very center of the good news of hope: The dead didn't stay dead, the decaying heart didn't keep decomposing, the deteriorating didn't keep disintegrating—and neither do we have to stay dead one moment longer.

Beyond the shadow of a doubt, it's verifiable, historical fact that whatever the women—the first preachers of the Resurrection—experienced, and whatever every other follower of Jesus experienced that Sunday morning and the days afterward, it was nothing less than life-giving and life-transformative and life-reorienting—to the extent they were willing to risk their very lives to proclaim it and fully live into the miracle of it: "The gospel is the royal announcement that the crucified and risen Jesus, who died for our sins and rose again according to the Scriptures, has been enthroned as the true Lord of the world."[1] If the stone turned back and a dead, divine Man walked out, then the whole of the world turns differently now, and who can now ever walk the same, breathe the same, love the same, live the same?

The sun turns differently now. The world spins differently, the soil over graves turns differently, your very heart turns differently now.

Because Jesus rose and turned that tombstone over, your every soul-crisis is forever over. And Jesus Christ is King and Lord forever over your life and days and moments now.

The reality is this all really happened, because if Jesus hadn't come out of that tomb, His name never would have come up again; if Jesus hadn't risen up from the dead, His name would never have gone down in history. Christianity only ever arose in the world because Jesus Christ literally rose up out of the grave. The only reason you've heard of Jesus is because women stood outside the tomb and heard these words: "Why do you seek the living among the dead? He is not here, but has risen" (Luke 24:5-6, ESV). What raised Christianity to the pinnacle of history is that Jesus was *bodily, literally raised from the dead*, and His resurrection is the last and surest sign that He is exactly who He says He is: the Way, the Truth, the Life.

John wrote about the first six signs to undeniably prove that this is all true, the divine love story of God-with-skin-on, who came to resurrect you to life in His love:

- The love revolution that turned water into wine at Cana (John 2:1-11)
- The love revolution that healed the official's son (John 4:46-54)
- The love revolution that restored the man lingering at the end of the pool of Bethsaida (John 5:2-9)
- The love revolution that multiplied five little loaves (John 6:1-14)
- The love revolution that smeared healing mud on the eyes of the man born blind (John 9:1-7)
- The love revolution that raised the decaying Lazarus (John 11:1-44)
- The ultimate love revolution of the Passion of God, when His love poured out to the nth degree on the Cross (John 19:1-37)

All these signs led up to the seventh and ultimate sign of divine Love coming passionately close, with a love absolutely out of this world: the Resurrection, the perfect Love that conquered death to win communion with us for forever.

Because the signs of Christ's otherworldly divinity are undeniable, and because He alone rose from the dead to kill death, it's unbelievably logical to make Him Lord of your life. If you've followed His whole story, seen the signs, seen His sacrifice at the Cross, seen the stone rolled away from the tomb, it follows that you would do nothing less than follow Him with your whole life.

The movement of real faith is always a resurrection movement in the heart.[2] To believe in the Resurrection is to believe there is a new way to be alive. This Love has come to actually love you to life—so you can live a life of supernatural love.

While these are the seven divine signs that might make you believe in the passionate love of God, who loves you into a new way of being, it's easy to be a Mary—Mary, who, though she was a passionate lover of God, still missed all the blazing signs. She missed what the startlingly empty tomb and what the folded shroud of God might mean. She entirely missed what the two angels in radiant white might mean. And, mistaking Him for the gardener, she completely missed that the risen, living, breathing Jesus was *standing right in front of her.*

Mary believed in the *general message* of Jesus, but she still completely missed the *deeply personal* message of Jesus. Even with all this undeniable evidence right in her face—that Jesus' love for her refused to die, that His love for her fiercely, miraculously, defiantly rose—Mary still kept looking around for a dead body, for the stench of a dead and rotting love. All Mary could see was catastrophic loss—when she was standing right in the center of a passionate love of the most cosmic proportions, which would make her a new creation!

Though Mary was bent over, broken with grief, blind to all the signs of undying love, in that very moment, God was restoring her and re-storying her, because God is always at work to turn everything in the world right around with His revolutionary love.

It's possible: You can feel abandoned right in the very spot where you are actually being loved to death, resurrected, restored, and re-storied into a completely new story.

Where God feels most absent in front of you may be exactly where God's presence is changing everything within you.

Where you only see the gardener with dirt under his fingernails, breaking up the soil of everything, there may actually be God, with your very name written on the palms of His hands, healing the heartbreak of everything.

It's reality now: Where you only see wreckage, God is working resurrection.

This is everything: The Resurrection is an empty tomb that holds every hope we have ever known.

Because "if Christ has not been raised, your faith is futile and you are still in your sins. . . . If in Christ we have hope in this life only, we are of all people most to be pitied. But in fact Christ has been raised from the dead, the firstfruits of those who have fallen asleep" (1 Corinthians 15:17, 19-20, ESV). Or, as *The Message* puts it, Christ is "the first in a long legacy of those who are going to leave the cemeteries."

Christ's resurrection and empty tomb are the sure hope that lifts the weight of every cross you've ever had to carry. Mary didn't yet know this when she was the only one who went to the tomb on the third morning; none of the other disciples even bothered to go look. Only Mary was ready to face violent grave robbers just to touch the face of her Lord. Mary's kind of love neutralized all kinds of fears. "Tell me where you have put him, and I will get him," Mary said to the man she thought was the gardener. Though she may have missed much, she was still full of much faith. She was so moved, so full of devotion to God, that she hadn't even considered: If she knew where His body was, was she actually filled with enough strength to move the dead body of God? Mary didn't think of how in the world she would carry a dead body—because all Mary wanted was God.

Love for God knows no load.

When you love the One who carried your cross so you could be carried into eternity, all your loads become lighter.

When your heart is heavy with love, everything done with love doesn't feel heavy.

When you have to have Jesus, you have all there is to really have.

While Mary may not have fully seen where God is, she nonetheless was still desperate for God. Yet it was only when Jesus clearly said her name that she could clearly see. Notably, Jesus didn't speak His name to Mary; rather, He spoke her own name to her.

Jesus reveals who He is—by revealing that He knows who you are.

When you come face-to-face with the death-defying, risen Jesus on Resurrection morning, can you believe that it's your very own name that finds itself announced in the cosmic Resurrection event?

Your name crosses the lips of the One whose lips cried out on the Cross.

God sees you, God knows you, and He looks you in the eye and says your name, because you are part of this resurrection story. You are stirred, you're stunned, you're remade—*and you are found*. Here, you recognize Him, here you see Him, here you discover your truest self, too, because never has your name been more charged with supernatural knowing and otherworldly love.

This is what Mary, the very first witness and evangelist, testified: "I have seen the Lord." Mary, John, and countless others witnessed, with their naked eye, very God on this very sod. That's what John always maintained was the essence of every word he wrote: "That which was from the beginning, which we have heard, which we have seen with our eyes, which we have looked at and our hands have touched—this we proclaim concerning the Word of life" (1 John 1:1-2).

Now that you have seen Him with your own eyes, what in your past could cast you away from speaking of Jesus now? Though Mary had seven demons cast out of her, that didn't cast her away from the joy of being the very first evangelist sent by the risen Savior—so how can you, too, not run and tell the world for all you're worth, because Jesus is worthy, because yesterday you were dead and *now you're alive*?

Now that we have seen Him, we will be like Him (1 John 3:2). Seeing the risen Christ is to be raised to be like Him.

To be fully alive . . . is to live fully like Him.

Jesus didn't go to the Cross so we could stay as we are. Jesus comes to the Cross *so we could become like Him*. You no longer belong to despair, to sickness, to failure, to death; you no longer belong to self or hopelessness or injustice or any dark story. You no longer are the walking numb, but you get to *live resurrection* by digging a hole to bury all the lies that you have to perform well enough to be loved, bury the scam that you have to earn your worth, bury the shame that you will never belong in the wide-open arms of God.

You belong to Jesus *to become like Jesus*. You belong to Love *to be love*. You belong to Hope *to raise hope*. You—your whole life—belongs in the hands that placed the stars, the hands that have your name forever etched right into the palms. And because Christ rises with His scars, with your name written right into His scars, Christ's rising is *your* rising.

Because Christ rises, still carrying His scars of suffering, then even—especially—we who are scarred and suffering get to be the rising people who rise to the fullest life, who live resurrections every day, who rise and run, fueled by the fire and passion of God.

Because Christ made His way out of that grave, there is now a way out of your every grave and out of every hopeless place into a new way of being human.

Here and now is your Lazarus moment too.

What was making you dead is now dead to you.

What was suffocating and strangling you is now finished for you.

You get to fold up all you've kept shrouded, and you get to walk out.

You get to lay down your skeletons and leave.

If the tomb wasn't empty, your hope would be.

If the tomb wasn't empty, your heart would be.

If the tomb wasn't empty, you would be.

But because the tomb is empty, your life isn't.

Because the tomb is now empty, your soul is always full, and you can live a truly fulfilling life.

Because of the Resurrection, we are no longer people of this earth, we are no longer people of death and dying, we are no longer people of this realm—we are now the rising people, we are people of the real Kingdom, we are people on pilgrimage with His presence, we are people of resurrection life—living in the very life of Christ Himself!

In the beginning was the Word, and the Word was Love, the only Love who has ever loved you to death and back to the realest, resurrected life that is found only in Him who is Life—and Life more abundantly.

Now the pilgrimage into enjoying new life together with Him forever . . . begins.

PERSONAL NOTES TO SOUL FROM TODAY'S PILGRIMAGE INTO THE HEART OF JESUS:

BECAUSE THE

TOMB IS EMPTY,

YOUR LIFE,

YOUR SOUL,

IS ALWAYS FULL.

NOTES

INTRODUCTION

1. Philip Schaff, "Latin Christianity: Its Founder, Tertullian," in *Ante-Nicene Fathers*, ed. Allan Menzies, Christian Classics Ethereal Library (Edinburgh: T&T Clark, 1885), https://ccel.org/ccel/schaff/anf03 /anf03.vi.vi.viii.html.

DAY 5: THIRSTY FOR GOD

1. *NLT Study Bible* (Carol Stream, IL: Tyndale House Publishers, 2017), 1772n.
2. Jonathan Edwards, "A Divine and Supernatural Light, Immediately Imparted to the Soul by the Spirit of God, Shown to Be Both Scriptural and Rational Doctrine," Monergism.com, https://www.monergism .com/thethreshold/articles/onsite/edwards_light.html.
3. Belden C. Lane, *Ravished by Beauty: The Surprising Legacy of Reformed Spirituality* (Oxford: Oxford University Press, 2011), 69.

DAY 7: A NEWBORN SOUL

1. Roland H. Bainton, *Here I Stand: A Life of Martin Luther* (New York: Meridian, 2015), 48.
2. Iain Murray, "Jonathan Edwards: The Life, the Man, and the Legacy," Desiring God, October 11, 2003, https://www.desiringgod.org/messages/jonathan-edwards-the-life-the-man-and-the-legacy.
3. Dane Ortlund, "5 Things Jonathan Edwards Teaches Us about the Christian Life," Crossway, August 26, 2014, https://www.crossway.org/articles/5-things-jonathan-edwards-teaches-us-about-the-christian-life/.

DAY 8: SOUL PARCHED

1. C. S. Lewis, *Mere Christianity* (New York: HarperOne, 2001), chapter 10.
2. Barbara Brown Taylor, "Identity Confirmation: John 4:5-42," The Christian Century, February 12, 2008, https://www.christiancentury.org/article/2008-02/identity-confirmation.

DAY 10: MADE WHOLE

1. Charles Haddon Spurgeon, "Jesus at Bethesda; or, Waiting Changed for Believing" (sermon, Metropolitan Tabernacle, Newington, England, April 7, 1867), the Spurgeon Center, https://www.spurgeon.org/resource -library/sermons/jesus-at-bethesda-or-waiting-changed-for-believing/#flipbook/.
2. John Calvin, *Commentary on the Gospel of John according to John*, trans. Rev. William Pringle, vol. 1 (Grand Rapids, MI: Christian Classics Ethereal Library), John 5:1-9, https://ccel.org/ccel/calvin/calcom34 /calcom34.xi.i.html.

DAY 11: BOUNTY

1. Leon Morris, *The Gospel According to John*, vol. 4, *The New International Commentary on the New Testament* (Grand Rapids, MI: Eerdmans, 1971), 342.

DAY 13: THE BREAD OF GOD

1. Alexander Schmemann, *For the Life of the World: Sacraments and Orthodoxy* (New York: St. Vladimir's Seminary Press, 1973), 17.

DAY 14: WHERE CAN YOU GO?

1. *Matthew Henry's Commentary*, John 6:60-71, https://www.biblegateway.com/resources/matthew-henry /John.6.60-John.6.71.

DAY 15: NOT CONDEMNED

1. Leon Morris, *The Gospel According to John*, vol. 4, *The New International Commentary on the New Testament* (Grand Rapids, MI: Eerdmans, 1971).
2. C. S. Lewis, "What Are We to Make of Jesus Christ?," in *God in the Dock: Essays on Theology and Ethics*, ed. Walter Hooper (Grand Rapids, MI: Eerdmans, 1970), 169, emphasis added.

DAY 16: LIGHT HAS DAWNED

1. Holly Otterbein, "If the Sun Went Out, How Long Would Life on Earth Survive?," *Popular Science*, October 20, 2008, https://www.popsci.com/node/204957/.
2. Henry Alford, *Greek Text Critical Exegetical Commentary*, John 8:1, https://biblehub.com /commentaries/alford/john/8.htm.
3. Charles Haddon Spurgeon, "The Light of the World" (sermon, Metropolitan Tabernacle, Newington, England, November 12, 1865), Christian Classics Ethereal Library, https://ccel.org/ccel/spurgeon /sermons62/sermons62.xlii.html.

DAY 17: WHY YOU?

1. Charles Haddon Spurgeon, "The Spur" (sermon, Metropolitan Tabernacle, Newington, England, July 31, 1870), the Spurgeon Center, https://www.spurgeon.org/resource-library/sermons/the-spur-2/#flipbook/.

DAY 18: KNOWN

1. Charles Haddon Spurgeon, "Our Own Dear Shepherd" (sermon, Metropolitan Tabernacle, Newington, England, November 26, 1885), The Spurgeon Center, https://www.spurgeon.org/resource-library/sermons /our-own-dear-shepherd/#flipbook/.

DAY 19: ONE

1. David Guzik, "John 10–The Good Shepherd," Enduring Word, https://enduringword.com/bible -commentary/john-10/.
2. John Stott, *The Cross of Christ* (Downers Grove, IL: InterVarsity Press, 1986), 159.
3. John Stott, *The Cross of Christ* (Downers Grove, IL: InterVarsity Press, 1986), chapter 6.
4. Eugene H. Peterson, *Eat This Book: A Conversation in the Art of Spiritual Reading* (Grand Rapids, MI: Eerdmans, 2006), xii.

DAY 22: PALMS OF PRAISE

1. Eli Lizorkin-Eyzenberg, *The Jewish Gospel of John: Discovering Jesus, King of All Israel* (Jewish Studies for Christians, 2019), 190.
2. Josephus, *Of the War*, 6.9.3, quoted in D. A. Carson, *The Gospel According to John*, vol. 4, *The Pillar New Testament Commentary* (Grand Rapids, MI: Eerdmans, 1991), 11, 130.
3. Simon Sebag Montefiore, *Jerusalem: The Biography* (New York: Knopf, 2011), 106.
4. "Exodus 12: God Institutes Passover," Enduring Word, https://enduringword.com/bible-commentary /exodus-12/.

DAY 23: LETTING GO

1. Charles Haddon Spurgeon, "The Corn of Wheat Dying to Bring Forth Fruit," *Farm Sermons*, The Spurgeon Archive, http://www.romans45.org/spurgeon/misc/corn.htm.

DAY 24: PEOPLE OF THE TOWEL

1. F. F. Bruce, *The Gospel of John: Introduction, Exposition, and Notes* (Grand Rapids, MI: Eerdmans, 1983).
2. Leon Morris, *The Gospel According to John*, vol. 4, *The New International Commentary on the New Testament* (Grand Rapids, MI: Eerdmans, 1971).

DAY 25: LOVING THE IMPOSSIBLE

1. Charles Haddon Spurgeon, "The New Park Street Pulpit" Volumes 1–6 and "The Metropolitan Tabernacle Pulpit" Volumes 7–63 (Pasadena, Texas: Pilgrim Publications, 1990).

DAY 26: THE WAY
1. Lesslie Newbigin, *The Gospel in a Pluralist Society* (Grand Rapids, MI: Eerdmans, 1989), 9–10.
2. Greg Koukl, "The Trouble with the Elephant," Stand to Reason, February 20, 2013, https://www.str.org/w/the-trouble-with-the-elephant.
3. Thomas à Kempis, *The Imitation of Christ* (New York: Dorset Press, 1952).

DAY 27: YOUR ADVOCATE
1. J. I. Packer, *Keep in Step with the Spirit* (Old Tappan, NJ: Fleming H. Revell, 1984), 66.

DAY 28: ABIDE
1. Andrew Murray, *Abide in Christ* (Radford, VA: Wilder Publications, 2008), preface.
2. C. S. Lewis, *The Complete C. S. Lewis Signature Classics* (San Francisco, CA: HarperSanFrancisco, 2002), 157.

DAY 30: AN UNTROUBLED HEART
1. William Barclay, *The Gospel of John*, vol. 2 (Louisville, KY: Westminster John Knox Press, 1975), https://www.studylight.org/commentaries/eng/dsb/john-16.html.

DAY 31: THE SAME PASSION
1. Saint Thérèse de Lisieux, *Story of a Soul: The Autobiography of Saint Therese of Lisieux* (Washington, DC: ICS Publications, 1976), 242.
2. Frederick Christian Bauerschmidt, *The Love That Is God: An Invitation to Christian Faith* (Grand Rapids, MI: Eerdmans, 2020), 82.
3. R. T. Kendall, *When God Shows Up: Staying Ready for the Unexpected* (Ventura, CA: Renew Books, 1998), 104.
4. F. F. Bruce, *The Gospel of John: Introduction, Exposition, and Notes* (Grand Rapids, MI: Eerdmans, 1983), 335–336.
5. "Saint Augustin on the Holy Trinity, Doctrinal Treatises, Moral Treatises," *A Select Library of the Nicene and Post-Nicene Fathers of the Christian Church*, vol. 3, ed. Philip Schaff (Buffalo, NY: The Christian Literature Co., 1887).

DAY 33: FOREVER BOUND TO YOU
1. Aryeh E. Shimron et al., "Petrochemistry of Sediment and Organic Materials Sampled from Ossuaries and Two Nails from the Tomb of the Family of the High Priest Caiaphas, Jerusalem," *Archaeological Discovery* 8, no. 3 (July 2020): 260–287, https://www.scirp.org/journal/paperinformation.aspx?paperid=101432.

DAY 37: THE REVOLUTIONARY CENTER
1. M. Tullius Cicero, *The Orations of Marcus Tullius Cicero*, trans. C. D. Yonge, vol. 1 (London: George Bell and Sons, 1903), 2.5.170.

DAY 38: PIERCED
1. Matthew Henry, *The Miscellaneous Writings of Matthew Henry*, vol. 7, *An Entire Collection of Matthew Henry's Works in Seven Volumes* (London: S. Bagster, 1811), 220.
2. John Stott, *The Cross of Christ* (Downers Grove, IL: InterVarsity Press, 1986), 159–160.
3. Paraphrase of fourth-century theologian John Chrysostom: "By the cross we know the gravity of sin and the greatness of God's love toward us."
4. John Donne, *The Major Works*, ed. John Carey (Oxford: Oxford University Press, 2000), 412.

DAY 39: SALVATION SATURDAY
1. Henri Nouwen, *A Letter of Consolation* (San Francisco: Harper and Row, 1989), 78, quoted in Nicholas Wolterstorff, *Lament for a Son* (London: Hodder and Stoughton, 1989), 87.

DAY 40: THE MOMENT EVERYTHING CHANGES
1. John Piper and N. T. Wright, "The Justification Debate: A Primer," comp. Trevin Wax, *Christianity Today* 53, no. 6 (June 2009): 34–35.
2. N. T. Wright, "Christian Origins and the Resurrection of Jesus: The Resurrection of Jesus as a Historical Problem," N. T. Wright Online, https://ntwrightpage.com/2016/07/12/christian-origins-and-the-resurrection-of-jesus-the-resurrection-of-jesus-as-a-historical-problem/.

ABOUT THE AUTHOR

ANN VOSKAMP is the wife of one fine farmer, mother to seven, and a four-time *New York Times* bestselling author of more than a dozen books, including *One Thousand Gifts: A Dare to Live Fully Right Where You Are* (which has sold more than 1.5 million copies and has been translated into more than twenty languages), *The Greatest Gift, Unwrapping the Greatest Gift, Waymaker,* and the critically acclaimed children's book *Your Brave Song.*

Named by *Christianity Today* as one of fifty women most shaping culture and the church today, Ann is a passionate advocate for the marginalized and oppressed around the globe, partnering with Mercy House Global, Compassion International, and artisans around the world through her fair trade community, Grace Case. She and her husband took a leap of faith to restore a 125-year-old stone church into The Village Table, a place where friends who are vulnerably housed are welcomed and everyone has a seat and belongs. Join the story at annvoskamp.com.

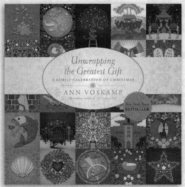

M THE LIGHT OF THE WOR

SHEPHERD ✠ I AM THE RES

THE TRUTH, AND THE LIF

AD OF LIFE ✠ I AM THE L

✠ I AM THE GOOD SHEPHE

LIFE ✠ I AM THE WAY, THE

E VINE ✠ I AM THE BREAD

RLD ✠ I AM THE DOOR ✠ I A

RESURRECTION AND THE L

E LIFE ✠ I AM THE TRUE V

E LIGHT OF THE WORLD ✠

HERD ✠ I AM THE RESURRE

E TRUTH, AND THE LIFE ✠

OF LIFE ✠ I AM THE LIGHT

AM THE BREAD OF LIFE + I

HE DOOR + I AM THE GOOD

ND THE LIFE + I AM THE W

HE TRUE VINE + I AM THE

HE WORLD + I AM THE DOO

HE RESURRECTION AND TH

ND THE LIFE + I AM THE TH

I AM THE LIGHT OF THE W

OOD SHEPHERD + I AM THE

HE WAY, THE TRUTH, AND

HE BREAD OF LIFE + I AM T

OOR + I AM THE GOOD SHE

HE LIFE + I AM THE WAY, T

RUE VINE + I AM THE BREA